What We Now Know

DISCARD

ALA Editions purchases fund advocacy, awareness, and
accreditation programs for library professionals worldwide.

College Libraries

and Student Culture

What We Now Know

EDITED BY
Lynda M. Duke
and Andrew D. Asher

AMERICAN LIBRARY ASSOCIATION
Chicago   2012

Printed in the United States of America

16   15   14   13   12   5   4   3   2   1

While extensive effort has gone into ensuring the reliability of the information appearing in this book, the publisher makes no warranty, express or implied, with respect to the material contained herein.

ISBN: 978–0-8389–1116-7 (paper); 978-0-8389-9357-6 (PDF); 978-0-8389-9358-3 (ePub); 978-0-8389-9359-0 (Mobipocket); 978-0-8389-9360-6 (Kindle). For more information on digital formats, visit the ALA Store at alastore.ala.org and select eEditions.

Library of Congress Cataloging-in-Publication Data

College libraries and student culture : what we now know / [edited by] Lynda M. Duke and Andrew D. Asher.
        p. cm.
    Includes bibliographical references and index.
    ISBN 978-0-8389-1116-7 (alk. paper)
    1. Ethnographic Research in Illinois Academic Libraries Project. 2. Academic
        libraries—Illinois—Use studies. 3. College students—Illinois—Attitudes.
        4. Academic libraries—Relations with faculty and curriculum—Illinois.
        5. Academic libraries—Services to minorities—Illinois. 6. Research—Methodology—
        Study and teaching (Higher)—Illinois. 7. Information behavior—Illinois—Case
        studies. 8. Libraries and colleges—Illinois—Case studies. 9. Libraries and students—
        Illinois—Case studies. 10. Libraries and teachers—Illinois—Case studies. I. Duke,
        Lynda M. II. Asher, Andrew D.
    Z675.U5C6458 2011
    027.7—dc23   2011032423

Book cover design by Casey Bayer. Text design in Charis SIL by Karen Sheets de Gracia. Composition by Dianne M. Rooney.

⊚ This paper meets the requirements of ANSI/NISO Z39.48-1992 (Permanence of Paper).

To my parents, Richard and Marie, for providing such wonderful opportunities throughout my life and for modeling the interwoven passions of education and lifelong learning.

To my husband, Diego, for bringing joy, adventures, and love into my life.

To my daughter, Victoria Lyudmila, the brightest, most beautiful and liveliest light in my world.

—LMD

For Sofiya and Alex, for their humor, and humoring me.

—ADA

CONTENTS

Acknowledgments   *ix*
ERIAL Project Research Teams   *xi*

1   **Ethnographic Research in Illinois Academic
    Libraries: The ERIAL Project**   *1*
    Andrew D. Asher, Susan Miller, and David Green

2   **Pragmatism and Idealism in the Academic
    Library: An Analysis of Faculty and Librarian
    Expectations and Values**   *15*
    Mary Thill

3   **Marketing the Library's Instructional Services to
    Teaching Faculty: Learning from Teaching Faculty
    Interviews**   *31*
    Annie Armstrong

4   **Why Don't Students Ask Librarians for Help?
    Undergraduate Help-Seeking Behavior in Three
    Academic Libraries**   *49*
    Susan Miller and Nancy Murillo

5   **Searching for Answers: Student Research
    Behavior at Illinois Wesleyan University**   *71*
    Andrew D. Asher and Lynda M. Duke

6   **Supporting the Academic Success of Hispanic Students**   *87*
David Green

7   **First-Generation College Students: A Sketch of Their Research Process**   *109*
Firouzeh Logan and Elizabeth Pickard

8   **Seeing Ourselves As Others See Us: Library Spaces through Student Eyes**   *127*
Jane Treadwell, Amanda Binder, and Natalie Tagge

9   **Transformative Changes in Thinking, Services, and Programs**   *143*
Lynda M. Duke

10   **Conclusions and Future Research**   *161*
Andrew D. Asher and Lynda M. Duke

APPENDIX
ERIAL Interview Guide Questions   *169*

Bibliography   *173*
Contributors   *185*
Index   *187*

ACKNOWLEDGMENTS

The ERIAL Project involved the hard work and dedication of many people. Above all, the ERIAL Project would never have occurred without the vision and commitment of David ("Dave") Green. With substantial support from Bradley Baker, dean of libraries and learning resources at Northeastern Illinois University, and Nancy Fried Foster, director of anthropological research for the University of Rochester's River Campus Libraries, Dave developed and submitted the research grant proposal in early 2008. While Dave was the chief principal investigator, his main role was that of project manager and overall cheerleader. All of us involved with the project are indebted to Dave for his leadership in bringing a complicated endeavor to its successful conclusion.

Nancy Fried Foster acted as project consultant throughout the two years of the grant, providing advice and assistance in planning the study, training the project librarians in ethnographic methods, adapting research instruments, and developing analysis strategies. The ERIAL Project members are most appreciative to Nancy, Susan Gibbons, and the research team at the River Campus Libraries of the University of Rochester for their willingness to share many of their research instruments. The ERIAL Project was fortunate to have Nancy and the University of Rochester's experience to build upon.

We are grateful for the grant awarded by the Illinois State Library, a department of the Office of the Secretary of State, which provided funding to the ERIAL Project through funds made available by the U.S. Institute of Museum and Library Services, under the federal Library Services and Technology Act (LSTA). We would also like to thank the Metropolitan Library System of Chicago for helping provide logistical and administrative support to the project.

Over 650 individuals participated in the ERIAL study, including students, librarians, and teaching faculty. We thank each of them for their time and willingness to answer questions, share ideas, draw maps, take photos, and be video-recorded. Without their contributions and commentaries, this project would not have been possible. It is our sincere hope that as a result of this project, and the direct involvement of so many individuals, the libraries and their services will play a more vital role on each of the five campuses.

Finally, we would like to thank all of the librarians and library staff who worked on the ERIAL Project, as well as the institutional research team members listed individually below. In many respects this was a labor of love. Research team members took on the work of the project in addition to their usual responsibilities and dedicated countless hours to this research, doing so with good humor, curiosity, and enthusiasm. A special thank-you is also due to the authors of the chapters in this book. We appreciate their diligence, hard work, and insights.

Andrew D. Asher

Lynda M. Duke

ERIAL PROJECT RESEARCH TEAMS

**Northeastern Illinois University
– Grant Awardee**
Dave Green – Project Manager
Lisa Wallis – Principal
　Investigator
Henry Owen
Jill Althage
Mary Thill
Nancy Murillo

DePaul University
Paula Dempsey – Principal
　Investigator
Beth Ruane
Elisa Addlesperger
Heather Jagman
Margaret Power (1st yr)
Missy Roser
Terry Taylor

Illinois Wesleyan University
Lynda Duke – Principal
　Investigator
Monica Moore (2nd yr)

Sue Stroyan
Suzanne Wilson
Lauren Dodge (1st yr)

University of Illinois at Chicago
Elizabeth Pickard – Co-Principal
　Investigator
Firouzeh Logan – Co-Principal
　Investigator
Annie Armstrong
LaVerne Gray (1st yr)
Lise McKean
Steve Brantley

**University of Illinois at
　Springfield**
Jane Treadwell – Principal
　Investigator
Alysia Peich (1st yr)
Amanda Binder (2nd yr)
Natalie Tagge (2nd yr)

Project Anthropologists
Andrew Asher
Susan Miller

1

Ethnographic Research in Illinois Academic Libraries: The ERIAL Project

ANDREW D. ASHER, SUSAN MILLER,
AND DAVID GREEN

R esearch assignments might seem to be one of the most routine and commonplace activities of university life. However, as students work within an information environment that is increasingly open and dynamically changing, research assignments also represent a complex and potentially daunting task. In order to examine this complexity, this book not only asks, "What are the practices and habits students employ to complete their academic research?" but also, "What are the expectations of teaching faculty and librarians for this research?" "What are the spaces in which students work and the tools they use?" and, centrally, "How can we understand the intricate web of interpersonal processes, transactions, and relationships that define the social landscape within which research is completed?"

These questions formed the impetus for the Ethnographic Research in Illinois Academic Libraries (ERIAL) Project, a 21-month research study conducted in 2008–2010 and funded by a Library Services and Technology Act grant through the Illinois State Library. The ERIAL Project investigated how university students conduct academic research and utilize library resources and services, and was organized around four core goals: to gain a better understanding of undergraduates' research processes based on firsthand accounts of how they obtained, evaluated, and managed information for their assignments; to explore how relationships between teaching faculty, librarians, and students shaped these processes; to assess the roles of academic libraries and librarians within students' research practices; and finally, to adjust library services to address students' needs more effectively. The ERIAL Project was a collaborative effort of the libraries at five Illinois universities: Northeastern Illinois University (NEIU), DePaul University, Illinois Wesleyan University (IWU), the University of Illinois at Chicago (UIC), and the University of Illinois at Springfield (UIS). As described in table 1.1, these universities ranged in size from just under 2,100 to over 26,000 students, and included campuses that were urban and suburban, residential and commuter, and public and private. As a

TABLE 1.1 *Characteristics of ERIAL Participant Universities. Enrollment figures, fall 2009. Source: U.S. Department of Education, Institute for Education Statistics, College Navigator (http://nces.ed.gov/collegenavigator/).*

	IWU	UIS	DePaul	UIC	NEIU
Location	Bloomington	Springfield	Chicago	Chicago	Chicago
Environment	Residential	Residential	Urban	Urban	Commuter/ Urban
Public/Private	Private	Public	Private	Public	Public
Type	Liberal Arts	Liberal Arts/ Professional	Research/ Catholic-Affiliated	Research	Hispanic-Serving
Total Enrollment	2,066	4,977	25,072	26,840	11,631
Undergraduate Enrollment	2,066	3,027	16,199	16,044	9,191
Graduate Enrollment	0	1,950	8,873	10,796	2,440

result of this diverse partnership, the ERIAL Project was able to query the similarities and differences of an array of library cultures. The ERIAL Project was built on an ethnographic methodology that employed a variety of anthropological data collection techniques to build a holistic, nuanced, and user-centered portrait of student needs through the observation of what students actually did while completing their research assignments. This approach yielded rich descriptions of students' experiences, including how they searched for information, the obstacles they encountered, the ways they sought help, their interactions with library spaces, and the effects of library instruction. In total, the ERIAL Project included more than 650 students, librarians, and faculty members participating in over 700 research activities, making it one of the largest and most comprehensive ethnographic investigations of library use to date, and providing detailed information about what research means to university students.

THE ETHNOGRAPHIC APPROACH

Ethnography is a collection of qualitative methods that focus on the close observation of social practices and interactions. Ethnography's unique contribution to qualitative research is that it deeply examines the context in which activities occur, usually involving a researcher working with participants as they go about their daily lives. Ethnographers typically describe a particular situation or process by asking multiple people about it, and by analyzing multiple types of data, such as interviews, direct observation, photographs, journals, or cultural artifacts. In this way, ethnography allows the researcher to see multiple interpretations of a situation. The ERIAL Project's ethnographic methods included semi-structured interviews, photo elicitation, participant observation in libraries, and mapping exercises, as well as other approaches. These methods are described in more detail below.

The ERIAL Project chose this type of qualitative research because it is especially well suited for elucidating complex processes—like research projects—that involve many steps and relationships, and for creating rich descriptions of individuals' experiences. Ethnographic research therefore tends to be inductive and theory-generating, that is, building an argument about how and why a particular process, practice, or event occurs based on empirical evidence. In this way, ethnography draws conclusions by examining individual observations to gradually construct a holistic picture of phenomena. This approach can have great explanatory power because it directly demonstrates what research subjects actually do, think, and feel in the midst of real-world situations.

Ethnographic methods facilitate in-depth and open-ended investigation into observed phenomena, allowing researchers a great deal of flexibility in pursuing research questions and enabling them to make fine distinctions between categories of experience. Ethnography also allows researchers to synthesize the social meaning of events and processes by triangulating from multiple viewpoints. This interpretive analysis yields rich descriptions of the ERIAL participants' research processes and needs in a way we hope will draw the reader into the user experience.

TABLE 1.2 *Demographic Characteristics of Undergraduate Students at ERIAL Participating Universities, fall 2009. Source: U.S. Department of Education, Institute for Education Statistics, College Navigator (http://nces.ed.gov/collegenavigator/).*

	IWU	UIS	DePaul	UIC	NEIU
Enrollment					
Full-Time	100%	65%	82%	93%	58%
Part-Time	0%	35%	18%	7%	42%
Age					
24 and Under	100%	58%	63%	89%	56%
Age 25 and Over	0%	42%	37%	11%	44%
Gender Ratio					
Male	41%	45%	45%	48%	42%
Female	59%	55%	55%	52%	58%
Race/Ethnicity					
Black/African American	5%	13%	9%	8%	10%
Hispanic/Latino(a)	3%	3%	13%	18%	30%
White/Caucasian	76%	72%	56%	44%	39%
Asian	5%	3%	8%	22%	10%
Unknown	7%	7%	11%	5%	7%

One potential drawback to the ethnographic approach is that it can sometimes be difficult to generalize qualitative data to a broader population, given its techniques for choosing participants and its open-ended methodological approach. For these reasons, when selecting participants for the ERIAL Project, we endeavored to choose individuals who reflected the diversity of the participating universities' student and faculty populations and range of research experiences (table 1.2). However, it remains prudent to use caution when interpreting ethnographic data to avoid over-generalization. For this reason, we refrain from making universal claims about the groups we studied (students, faculty, and librarians). Instead we seek to explain and interpret the patterns we observed in our data, and, whenever possible, to allow our respondents to speak in their own words.

ERIAL STUDY BACKGROUND

The ethnographic study of libraries is a relatively new and developing field of applied anthropology. Despite a call for increased use of ethnography in library and information science research by Sandstrom and Sandstrom (1995), prior to 2000 few studies had applied ethnographic approaches to either libraries or student research practices (a few exceptions include Crabtree et al. [1997, 1998, 2000], Forsyth [1998], Nahl [1998], and Seadle [2000]).[1] Ethnographic studies of university students in general are similarly limited (see Shumar 2004), and while this work has produced several now-classic monographs, including Michael Moffatt's study (1989) of students at Rutgers University, *Coming of Age in New Jersey*, and Dorothy Holland and Margaret Eisenhart's study (1990) of undergraduate women, *Educated in Romance,* it is now showing its pre-Internet age. More recently, Susan Blum's (2009) *My Word!* makes an ethnographic examination of plagiarism in student assignments, while Cathy Small's (writing as Rebekah Nathan) *My Freshman Year* gives an account of student life at Northern Arizona University based on her own experience enrolling as a "returning" student (Nathan 2005), a study which is unfortunately plagued by methodological and ethical issues stemming from Small's decision to conceal her identity from the students she investigated.

Interest in using ethnography to understand library users' needs and behaviors continued to increase in the mid-2000s (see Bryant 2007, 2009; Foster and Gibbons 2005; Jahn 2008; Ostrander 2008; Othman 2004; and

Suarez 2007), and the first large-scale ethnographic study of how students utilize the library was conducted in 2004–2006 by Nancy Fried Foster and Susan Gibbons at the University of Rochester (Foster and Gibbons 2007). The success of this study in uncovering the details of student life encouraged many librarians to apply similar methods to their own libraries, and inspired a number of studies of student research processes and library use, including projects at the Massachusetts Institute of Technology (Gabridge, Gaskell, and Stout 2008) and Wesleyan University (Hobbs and Klare 2010), as well as a major study at Fresno State University (Delcore, Mullooly, and Scroggins 2009) and the ERIAL Project itself.

The initial idea for the ERIAL Project was formed in 2007 when David Green, associate university librarian for collections and information services at the Ronald Williams Library of Northeastern Illinois University, heard Nancy Fried Foster and Dave Lindahl speak at the Library and Information Technology Association's National Forum about the University of Rochester study. Impressed with their work, Green collaborated with colleagues from the University of Illinois at Chicago and DePaul University to pursue a diverse, multisite study design. In order to diversify and enrich the study even more, two additional universities located in central Illinois were invited to join: Illinois Wesleyan University and the University of Illinois at Springfield. Funding was secured through the Illinois State Library, a department of the Office of the Secretary of State, via a Library Services and Technology Act grant. After a series of discussions, Foster agreed to participate as a consultant in the design and development of the proposal and project.

Each of the five libraries in the ERIAL Project was charged with forming its own library research team, which consisted of a designated lead research librarian and several other library faculty or staff members. The project required two full-time anthropologists: one to serve the three Chicago-area libraries and another to work with the two central Illinois libraries. Green acted as the grant coordinator and project manager. Defining roles and expectations was critical in a project that was conducted across five institutions and half the state of Illinois. Figure 1.1 presents a representation of the organizational structure used by the project.

The ERIAL Project was designed with a modular structure so that the five participating libraries could work independently. Each library's research team consisted of three to six members. The lead research librarian served as the point person for the team and reported to the coordinating

The ERIAL Project: Ethnographic Research in Illinois Academic Libraries

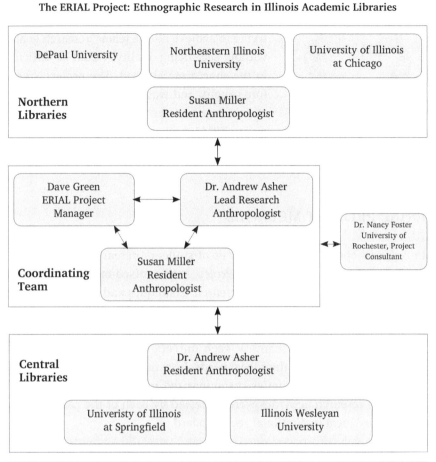

FIGURE 1.1 *The ERIAL Project Organization*

team, which consisted of the project manager and the two anthropologists, with Andrew Asher assuming primary responsibility for ensuring the overall integrity of the project's research methods as the lead research anthropologist.

The research was structured so that no one institution was dependent on another institution. If an institution found that during the course of the project it was no longer able to participate for any reason, it would not threaten the completion of the entire project. In a sense, ERIAL consisted of five simultaneous projects sharing a common core of research questions and methods. This structure is illustrated by figure 1.2.

FIGURE 1.2
The ERIAL Project Structure

While the ERIAL Project was initially funded for nine months, it became clear that trying to achieve all the teams' research goals, without sacrificing quality, would be difficult in the short time allotted. The project therefore sought, and was awarded, a second year of funding from the State Library of Illinois, giving ERIAL a 21-month project period.

ERIAL PROJECT METHODS

In order to obtain a holistic portrait of students' research practices and academic assignments, the ERIAL Project used a mixed-methods approach that integrated nine qualitative research techniques and was designed to generate verbal, textual, and visual data.[2] While all five participating institutions committed to a core set of research questions and shared research protocols, the research teams at each university chose which methods would be best suited for their local needs. Institutional participation in the nine ERIAL research activities is summarized in table 1.3 and discussed below. All research activities were reviewed by each of the participating universities' local institutional review board.

Ethnographic interviews were conducted with 156 students, 75 teaching faculty, and 49 librarians to elicit each group's understanding of their role in the student research process and their expectations for the other groups during student research. The interviews were conducted by a project anthropologist (or, in the case of some student interviews, a librarian) and lasted approximately 45 to 60 minutes. The interviews followed a common structure and utilized open-ended questions intended to elicit specific examples describing students' experiences undertaking research assignments, as well as how librarians and faculty members interacted with students during the research process (see appendix A). Questions focused on each group's understanding of students' previous preparation for research, elements of good research projects, major themes of the research process, how students sought help, obstacles that students faced, librarians' and students' experiences of working together, and librarians'

TABLE 1.3 *Participation in ERIAL Project Research Activities*

	DePaul	IWU	NEIU	UIC	UIS	TOTAL
Librarian Interviews	9	9	13	13	5	49
Librarian Photo Journals	7	5	6	N/A	3	21
Faculty Interviews	14	15	16	15	15	75
Student Interviews	32	30	27	32	35	156
Student Photo Journals	11	13	11	11	10	56
Student Mapping Diaries	N/A	24	10	N/A	N/A	34
Students in Web Design Workshops	N/A	30	20	N/A	N/A	50
Faculty in Web Design Workshops	N/A	4	8	N/A	N/A	12
Librarians/Staff in Web Design Workshops	N/A	15	9	N/A	N/A	24
Research Process	10	30	10	10	N/A	60
Student Cognitive Maps	37	44	33	N/A	23	137
Student Research Journals	N/A	17	N/A	N/A	N/A	17
Retrospective Research Paper Interview	N/A	9	N/A	N/A	N/A	9
Student Space Design Workshops	N/A	N/A	N/A	N/A	19	19
TOTAL	120	245	163	81	110	719

and faculty members' experiences of, and hopes for, working together. Faculty and students were also asked to recall in detail a recent research assignment and to describe their roles in it.

Photo journals were completed with 56 students and 21 librarians. Each respondent was loaned a digital camera and asked to take a set of 25 photos over the course of several days. These photos included views of work spaces, communication and computing devices, books, and favorite work/study locations. After participants took the photos, follow-up interviews were conducted by a project anthropologist (with librarians and some of the student participants) or a project librarian (with some of the student participants). Interviews elicited responses to the contents of the photos to learn about the processes and tools students used to complete their research assignments and to learn about the context in which their research happened. *Mapping diaries* were completed with 34 students. Each respondent was given a set of maps of her campus and was asked to mark her movements over the course of one academic day, noting the times and places she visited and the purpose for going there. Afterward, the project anthropologist conducted a brief interview with the student to debrief the day's events. The maps elicited more information about the spaces in which students conducted their research and day-to-day schoolwork.

Research journals were completed with 17 students. In the research journals activity, each participant was given a notebook at the beginning of a semester and asked to make an entry every time he worked on a research assignment. These entries were to include the date, time, place of work, and brief description of the type of activity the student was doing. The researchers then collected the completed journals at the end of the semester.

Web design workshops were conducted with students, faculty, and librarians. Five student design workshops (50 students combined), two faculty workshops (12 faculty combined), and three librarian/staff workshops (24 librarians/staff combined) elicited participants' opinions on the design and content of the library home page. Participants were asked a series of brainstorming questions to generate the features that would be included on a "perfect" library website, and were asked to mark up a printed screenshot of the library's home page with what they liked and disliked, and what they might like to see changed. Participants were then grouped into teams and asked to design from scratch their ideal home pages using large tablets of paper. Finally, respondents presented their ideal designs to each other and discussed the web page as a large group.

Space design workshops were conducted with 19 students. Similar to the web design workshops, this activity elicited participants' opinions on the design of the library's physical space. Participants were asked a series of brainstorming questions about the tasks and activities they completed in the library, which characteristics of the library they liked and disliked, and what they might like to see changed. Participants were then asked to design a perfect library space from scratch on a large piece of paper and to present their ideal designs to the group.

Cognitive maps were completed with 137 students. Over a series of several days, the project anthropologists solicited students' participation in cognitive mapping at several locations across the ERIAL campuses. Participants completed this activity away from the library itself, so that their results would not be affected by immediate visual cues. To complete the cognitive mapping exercise, the respondent was given a blank piece of paper with short directions at the top, along with blue, green, and red pens. Students were then given six minutes to draw a map of the library from memory, and asked to change the color of their marker every two minutes, an approach that allowed the researchers to learn which elements of the map students drew first, second, and third, and provided both spatial and temporal data about how students conceptualized library spaces.

Research process interviews were conducted with 60 students. Participants were asked to allow a project anthropologist to accompany them while they conducted research for an assignment. The anthropologist videotaped the student as she worked and asked clarifying questions about her research processes and approaches. Interviews averaged approximately 15 to 30 minutes. This firsthand observation facilitated a rich understanding of how exactly students conducted their search for information.

Retrospective research paper interviews were conducted with 9 students. In the retrospective research paper interview, participants were asked to give a step-by-step account of how they completed a previous research assignment while drawing each step on a large sheet of paper, producing both a narrative and a visual account of the assignment from beginning to end.

Student participants in the ERIAL study were recruited via e-mails, outreach at campus activity fairs, by approaching students in student unions, through online surveys and presentations in classes, and referrals through friends. Faculty members were recruited via general e-mails, as well as targeted telephone calls and e-mails to those who were identified as assigning research projects in their classes, including specific individuals who had requested library instruction in the previous year and those who had not. All librarians providing reference and instruction at each of the participating libraries were also contacted via e-mail and telephone. In most cases, students were given a gift certificate (typically a $10 value) as an incentive for participation, although for some activities (such as the design workshops and cognitive maps) students were provided with lunch or snacks as a thank-you for participating. Faculty members and librarians were not given incentives for participation.

ERIAL ANALYSIS STRATEGIES

After transcribing the research activities, the library research teams coded the transcripts using a modified version of grounded theory, an approach that allows interpretive themes and research conclusions to arise directly from the data (see Glaser and Strauss 1967; Bryant and Charmaz 2010).[3] Via a structured, team-based method, each research team brainstormed what students, teaching faculty, and librarians were doing during various parts of the student research process (e.g., getting help, facing obstacles, searching for information) and what expectations each group had of the others, with the goal of elucidating patterns within the research data. Team members and the anthropologists also wrote memos about what they were learning, and an analysis document was created at the end of each brainstorming session to capture the discussion. Qualitative analysis software assisted in this process as anthropologists applied codes generated in team discussion to the data and created additional codes. This process proceeded iteratively as teams analyzed sections of data and compared findings from one population to another. Site reports summarizing findings preserved analyses long-term and facilitated cross-site comparisons of data.

The research teams also spent a great deal of time, as a group, watching the video recordings of the research interviews, in order to assist with analyses. This "co-viewing" process helped determine what additional questions the research team would like to ask during the ethnographic interviews, and also allowed the teams to link the data from students' interviews to photographs and maps created during photo journal and mapping diary exercises (for a model of the co-viewing process, see Foster and Gibbons 2007, 55–58). Co-viewings with other members of library staff brought additional insights to the analysis, as well as providing a useful vehicle for explaining the research team's work to nonparticipating library faculty and staff and inviting investment in the project from the library at large.

The research teams used a number of processes to generate actionable service changes. At each brainstorming meeting, the research teams generated service ideas based on needs that appeared in the data. At the end of analysis, some teams created master lists of potential service changes, ranking them based on their importance and feasibility, to begin to think about which service changes to implement.

In order to respond to the user needs identified during the analysis process, research teams also brainstormed possible solutions, working with their colleagues in the library and beyond to determine which of these solutions were important and feasible to implement. To date, teams' analysis processes are driving service changes in a number of areas. For example, since faculty often act as gatekeepers to students' relationships with the library and librarians, a number of ERIAL libraries hosted colloquia with their faculty to review project findings together and begin to address how they might improve their collaboration as they assist students during research.

Finally, site reports were presented to libraries' administrations to facilitate discussion of service changes, and most of the institutions also presented their findings to other members of library staff.

ORGANIZATION OF THIS STUDY

This book presents a selection of the most salient findings about teaching faculty, librarians, and students from the five ERIAL universities. In chapter 2, Mary Thill examines how differences in faculty and librarian values and attitudes toward higher education at UIC and DePaul affect their expectations for students' research. Chapter 3 focuses on faculty-librarian relationships, with Annie Armstrong using data from ERIAL faculty interviews to evaluate how librarians can better address teaching faculty's needs for research instruction. Chapter 4 shifts our analytical focus to students, as Susan Miller and Nancy Murillo ask how students seek help with academic assignments and why so few utilize librarians. In chapter 5, Andrew Asher and Lynda Duke make a detailed exploration of how IWU students search for information and the myriad problems and difficulties they encounter as they locate academic resources. In chapter 6, David Green examines the needs of Latino and Latina students at NEIU and evaluates how the library can best support this student group. Similarly, Firouzeh Logan and Elizabeth Pickard focus on the particular needs and research practices of first-generation college students at UIC in chapter 7. In chapter 8, Jane

Treadwell, Amanda Binder, and Natalie Tagge relate UIS's experience in using ethnographic methods to inform a master plan for a redesign and renovation of their library. Finally in chapter 9, Lynda Duke demonstrates how ethnographic data can be used to generate library service changes and policy recommendations.

Together, these chapters represent a cross section of the depth and breadth of the ERIAL Project, as well as the complexity of relationships, processes, and practices that shape the meanings, experiences, and outcomes of students' academic research. While no study is exhaustive, it is our hope that these chapters will help to illuminate what it means to be a university student, faculty member, or librarian, as well as inspire additional ethnographies that continue to explore the diversity of university life.

NOTES

1. Sandstrom and Sandstrom's article sparked a five-year debate in *The Library Quarterly* on the epistemological and methodological underpinnings of ethnographic research (see Epperson 2006, 5–6; Nyce and Thomas 1999; Sandstrom and Sandstrom 1998, 1999; Thomas and Nyce 1998). Given that the arguments framing this debate relied on theoretical positions that were unlikely to be readily accessible to a nonanthropologist, this debate probably did little to encourage the use of ethnography in library research.

2. The photo journals, mapping diaries, web design workshops, space design workshops, and retrospective research paper interviews were adapted from protocols developed by Nancy Foster and the "Studying Students" research team at the River Campus Libraries of the University of Rochester. The ERIAL Project would like to express its appreciation to Nancy Fried Foster, Susan Gibbons, and the members of the University of Rochester research team for sharing these protocols with our project. For more information on the University of Rochester study, see Foster and Gibbons (2007).

3. For a more extensive discussion of ERIAL's ethnographic analysis process, see Asher and Miller (2010).

2

Pragmatism and Idealism in the Academic Library: An Analysis of Faculty and Librarian Expectations and Values

MARY THILL

President Barack Obama has called education "the economic issue of our time." Noting that the United States has recently fallen to twelfth place in college graduation rates for young adults, he warns, "The countries that out-educate us today will out-compete us tomorrow" (Shear 2010). While many in higher education welcome the president's proposals to expand Pell grants and student tax credits, not everyone supports his vocational view of education. In fact, there is a long-standing debate about the purpose of a university education. The battling factions are, on one side, what I would call the *pragmatists*, who look to the academy to train the American workforce and to enrich society, and on the other side, the *idealists*, who support the liberal-progressive view that the university is about self-actualization and the creation and dissemination of ideas.

Today's idealists find themselves at odds with an increasingly pragmatic student body. According to the most recent *Profile of Today's College Student,* which surveys undergraduates throughout the United States, 25 percent of students report that their main reason for wanting to earn a college degree is to make a good salary after graduation, and another 53 percent name career plans or the desire to move ahead in life as their primary motivation. In contrast, just 6 percent of college students want to earn a degree because they "like to learn for learning's sake" (NASPA Foundation 2008). Furthermore, the number of liberal arts degrees conferred in recent years lags behind vocational degrees. For example, in 2007, American universities conferred 350,000 bachelor's degrees in business, compared to approximately 150,000 degrees in communications and the visual and performing arts (U.S. Department of Education).

From the librarian and faculty perspective, whether we are pragmatists or idealists affects our preferred models of student research. A pragmatic view of education suggests that we understand student motivation as tied to the academy's reward system (i.e., grades) and economic or vocational incentives. We expect students to "satisfice" in their research, investing only enough effort to make the grade. In contrast, an idealistic view of education suggests that we believe students should be motivated by a love of learning. We expect student researchers to invest a significant amount of time in contemplation and discovery. The role of the academic librarian is different in each scenario. In the first, the librarian treats the student as a customer, whereas in the second, the librarian plays the role of guide or educator.

In this chapter, I analyze ethnographic interviews of faculty and librarians at two Chicago-area universities, DePaul University and Northeastern Illinois University, with an eye for participant idealism and pragmatism. In particular, I am interested in the interplay of faculty and librarian values and in areas of conflict or inconsistency. It is my belief that a better understanding of faculty and librarian pragmatism and idealism will help academic librarians to improve their outreach and make user-centered decisions regarding library services, resources, and programs.

BACKGROUND

> Any institution of education gains social legitimacy only by fulfilling the specific responsibility of providing the next generation with the capacities, beliefs, and commitments thought necessary to ensure society's goals. (Shapiro 2005, 37–38)

Although former Princeton president Harold Shapiro and others urge members of the academy to engage in dialogue to examine the role of higher education in society, my research revealed few such discussions in the library literature. In the late 1990s and at the turn of the millennium, a host of research papers, such as Dole and Hurych's "Values for Librarians in the Information Age" (2001) and "Ethical Values of Information and Library Professionals: An Expanded Analysis" by Koehler et al. (2000) advanced the study of librarian values. Using survey instruments to compare the values of librarians in different professions, in different geographic regions, and at different stages of their careers, these studies pose the question, "What values do all librarians share?" In "Point. Click. Matriculate: Corporate Influence in the University and the Academic Library," Joyce Weaver (1999) outlines the potential threats of pragmatism to academic libraries. However, previous articles omit a study of the fundamental pragmatic and idealistic values of academic librarians.

In popular literature and educational publications, the purpose of higher education has been enthusiastically debated for more than a century. Cardinal Newman, in his influential 1858 collection entitled *The Idea of a University,* introduced modern audiences to the liberal-idealist model of education, writing, "I am asked what is the end of University Education, and of the Liberal or Philosophical Knowledge which I conceive it to impart . . . Knowledge is capable of being its own end. Such is the constitution of the human mind, that any kind of knowledge, if it be really such, is its own reward" (Newman 2007, 102–3). Thus, idealists believe the greatest object of a university education is self-actualization.

Contemporary idealists promote Newman's conception of higher education. In "College and the Well-Lived Life," former Harvard president Derek Bok promotes individual self-fulfillment as the most important aim of higher education. "Educators and policy makers must recognize that there is much more to education than becoming a productive member of the workforce—and more to universities than producing 'human capital.' Happiness remains the ultimate end to which other goals are only the means" (Bok 2010, A37). Idealists resist attempts to quantify the value of higher education, as novelist Mark Slouka explains:

> Consider the ritual of addressing our periodic "crises in education." Typically, the call to arms comes from the business community. We're losing our competitive edge, sounds the cry . . . The president swings into action. He orders up a blue-chip commission of high-ranking business executives . . . to study the problem and come up with "real world" solutions. Thus empowered, the commission crunches the numbers, notes the depths to which we've sunk, and emerges into the light to underscore the need for more accountability. To whom? Well, to business, naturally. To whom else would you account? (Slouka 2009, 36)

Idealists argue that instruments of outcomes measurement reduce education to a simple business proposition.

Pragmatists value higher education for its potential to transform society and the economy. They note that vocations with higher earning potential require college, if not graduate-level, education. In "Do We Need More College Graduates?" social science professor William Beaver draws on statistics from the Bureau of Labor Statistics to link baccalaureate degree completion and earning potential, comparing the $1,140 weekly salary of an average college graduate to the $630 weekly salary of the average high school graduate (2010, 309). He notes that more members of lower income groups will need a college education if we are to create a "more affluent, cohesive, and stable society" (Beaver 2010, 311).

Citing the growing personal and financial responsibilities placed on students, pragmatists look for the academy to justify the investment. Indeed, approximately 63 percent of American undergraduates report working for pay during the academic year, with 58 percent working 16 hours a week or more. A substantial portion of students work to support themselves and/or their families (19 percent) (NASPA Foundation 2008). Nonetheless, the leading reason students work is to pay for some or all of their college and personal expenses (47 percent) (NASPA Foundation 2008). This is due, in part, to the rising price of higher education. In 1980, the average annual cost of undergraduate tuition, fees, room, and board was $3,101. Ten years later in 1990, that figure had more than doubled to $6,562. In 2007, the most recent year available, the costs had ballooned to $16,245 (U.S. Department of Education). Adjusting for inflation through the Consumer Price Index, these figures indicate a 51 percent increase in the cost of higher education from 1980 and an increase of 67 percent from 1990 (U.S. Department of Labor).

The language in the Information Literacy Competency Standards, published by the Association of College and Research Libraries (ACRL), suggests that librarians support both the pragmatic and liberal views of higher education.

> Because of the escalating complexity of this environment, individuals are faced with diverse, abundant information choices—in their academic studies, in the workplace, and in their personal lives . . . Developing lifelong learners is central to the mission of higher education institutions. By ensuring that individuals have the intellectual abilities of reasoning and critical thinking, and by helping them construct a framework for learning how to learn, colleges and universities provide the foundation for continued growth throughout their careers, as well as in their roles as informed citizens and members of communities. (Association of College and Research Libraries 2000)

The expression "in their academic studies, in the workplace, and in their personal lives" acknowledges the vocational applications of higher education (information literacy is important to the successful workplace), as well as the liberal view (information literacy is necessary to the student experience and enriches students' personal lives). The mandate to develop lifelong learners answers the missions of liberal and vocational education, while the ACRL answers pragmatists' calls for stricter accountability by drawing up specific learning goals and objectives.

METHODS

Thirty faculty and nine librarian transcripts from DePaul and NEIU were reviewed. The interviews took the form of a series of open-ended questions to reveal faculty and librarian expectations for the student research process.

Other librarians who have utilized qualitative methods to examine faculty values have noted the advantages of this method: "The open-ended questions used in the study are purposefully broad, in contrast to the focused nature of the study's quantitative measures, in order to provide an opportunity for respondents to introduce concepts or attitudes not anticipated by the predefined structure of the quantitative measures" (McClanahan 2010, 211). As I looked for common themes in the interviews, I discovered frequent references to pragmatism and idealism. I reread and coded the transcripts to explore this topic.

In my analysis, I excluded no part of the thirty-nine interviews. Nevertheless, I found myself returning to the following questions for the richness of relevant data:

- What are the elements of a good research project?
- What do you think students expect of librarians?
- What do you think faculty expect of librarians?
- What is the librarian role in ensuring students' success?
- If you could change one or two things about the students, what would they be?

These questions deal with faculty and librarian experiences, ideals, and expectations for and during the research process.

This study is exploratory, especially given some limitations of the data. As the principal focus of the ERIAL study was not the perceived mission of higher education, interviews did not include specific questions that might have revealed more about participants' values. Also, in the open-ended retrospective interviews, not every participant was asked exactly the same set of questions. Therefore, the portrait I draw may not be entirely complete. Another problem is the small sample size for this study, since NEIU librarians chose to seal their interviews for confidentiality reasons, limiting this portion of my analysis to DePaul librarians. It is possible that a larger study of librarian interviews would not reveal the same kind of consensus that I found in faculty interviews. At the conclusion of this chapter, I make recommendations for further study to address these and other limitations.

DISCUSSION

"The University Is Not What It Used to Be"

ANTHROPOLOGIST: If you could change one or two things about to-day's students, what would it be?

FACULTY MEMBER: A greater curiosity and a greater interest . . . I think the university is changing what the university education is . . . The university is not what it used to be. I think that students, whether it's undergrads and grads, see it as a hoop. And so it's sort of intellectual curiosity which I think feeds research and is not what it used to be and so if there's anything I could change about students it would be that . . . And along with that comes a decreased interest really in devoting oneself to learning what it takes to be able to do research effectively, write well, and so forth.

Most professors in the ERIAL study supported the liberal understanding of the mission of the university. Participants regularly chose words and phrases like *exploration, learning for its own sake, discovery,* and *persistence* to describe their ideal model of student research. Furthermore, faculty affirmations of their own idealistic values were often accompanied by censure of student pragmatism, as in the following comment. "Maybe this is just a sign of the times [but] there's this lack of patience with exploring ideas for the sake of exploring ideas. It seems like a lot of our students tend to think that the point of education is to get employment credentials. . . . I don't think that's the point of education." In such excerpts, vocational-minded students appeared intellectually lazy or apathetic.

In general, librarians also favored the idealistic view of higher education. Participants used terms like *curious* and *persistent* positively, and terms like *grade-driven* and *satisficing* pejoratively. The following excerpt includes the most explicit statement of idealism in a librarian interview.

ANTHROPOLOGIST: If you could change one or two things about the students, what would it be?

LIBRARIAN: Oh, poor students. They're under . . . a tremendous amount of stress. And having, having less financial pressure. And

having better time management skills. And this is idealistic, but having a less instrumental view of education, so, yeah.

ANTHROPOLOGIST: Instrumental in what way?

LIBRARIAN: In terms of, what is the minimum I need? And this may
have to do with time pressure and financial pressure too, but what
is the minimum I can do to get through this assignment, rather than
having the sense of intellectual ownership for wanting to learn something new.

Repeating a common theme, the participant associated the pragmatic
understanding of education with a resistance to fulfill any but the "minimum" assignment requirements.

However, librarians lacked the faculty's consensus on the liberal mission of higher education. Perhaps this is because LIS degrees have a more
professional orientation. Additionally, academic librarians must serve
liberal faculty members and pragmatic students, as well as vocational
programs within the university. In defining the librarian's role in ensuring student success, a librarian said, "I think we're all here to support
the ultimate academic mission of the university, which is that students
should come out, whatever their education, whether it's a professional
education or a liberal arts education, they come out with certain learning
goals." Note that the librarian took care to reference both the vocational
("professional education") and idealist ("liberal arts education") goals of
higher education.

Nonetheless, idealistic librarians and faculty shared in nostalgia for
what I will call the "golden age of higher education," an unspecified time in
the past when students entered the university to pursue knowledge for its
own sake. For instance, a librarian said, "I feel like sometimes [students] go
into this instant gratification culture which we have now where everything
is really fast. And if you don't get what you need immediately, you just give
up." Another questioned some students' commitment to "the enterprise of
education." These, and other similar comments, are alternative ways of
saying that "the university is not what it used to be."

Interestingly, the largely mythical idea of a golden age of education has
a long history. Some eighty years ago, William Wistar Comfort, president

of Haverford College, was quoted in an editorial for the *Saturday Evening Post* saying,

> [We are in the midst of] the deepest heart searching that American education has undergone. There are now said to be upward of a million students in our colleges and universities . . . Everything has been done to encourage numbers; entrance has been made easy, inducements have been extended, material and social advantages have been emphasized. College life has become attractive, if not for educational reasons, at least for many other reasons. True education has been seriously jeopardized. As a result, our institutions of higher learning have been overwhelmed, not with scholars but with amiable bipeds . . . They have been allowed to study what they please. ("What's a College for?" 1932)

Comfort's remarks echo the concerns of the idealistic faculty and librarians in the ERIAL study: students are interested only in the pragmatic benefits of higher education. The curriculum is not rigorous enough. The true mission of education (i.e., the liberal-progressive model) is in decline.

The shared ideals of liberal education mean that faculty and librarians described a successful research project in similar ways. I had expected librarians to focus more on the selection and attribution of appropriate resources, while faculty would preoccupy themselves with the form and content of student research. Instead, I identified eight criteria common to both faculty and librarian descriptions of a good research paper.[1] In addition, I found two highly relevant themes to a discussion of pragmatism and idealism: the idea that research must be a time-consuming endeavor, and the idea that research must be difficult.

"I Feel Like It's Not a Fast Process a Lot of Times"

ANTHROPOLOGIST: If you could change one or two things about to-day's students, what would it be?

LIBRARIAN: I wish [students] would be more persistent or less daunted by things, like, to stick with it. Some of them have really good stick-to-itiveness, so I don't mean to say that they don't. They're all really busy. They work and they go to school and they run around and stuff . . . But I wish there was a way for them to have more time to think through things. I feel like it's not a fast process a lot of times.

Like the participant in the above quotation, faculty members and librarians described the successful research process as time-consuming. A professor urged commuter students to "spend time at home . . . A lot of the thinking has to occur at home, off campus." In analyzing a recent batch of disappointing graduate papers, another faculty member attributed poor student performance to rushed research. "[Students] turned in assignments where they quite obviously could have done more or could have thought about it more carefully . . . Altogether maybe speed or lack of time is one of the issues." Repeatedly, librarians and professors wished that students could invest more time in contemplation and discovery, painting an idealized portrait of students leisurely wandering the stacks or pensively sitting down to await inspiration.

Faculty and librarian participants recognized that students must often adopt a pragmatic view of their education to cope with personal and financial pressures. In a discussion of student procrastinators, a professor of biology commented, "I really think that a lot of our student body is just so stretched. I mean, they work full-time, try to go to school, have family obligations. And . . . a lot of them would do it earlier if there was time for them to do it. But many of them just have their plates full." A librarian expressed a similar view, "[The students are] pretty tired a lot of the time. You can see that . . . I know exactly what that feels like. I've done three degrees and I know what it feels like to have pressure, assignments, multiple deadlines, and all the rest of it . . . They want to learn, they want to do a good paper. It's not that they don't care." Participants understood that the idealistic model of slow, deliberate research is unattainable for many students.

Though sympathetic, the professors interviewed described few concessions that they had made for time-pressed and pragmatic students. Rather, they placed the onus on the students to carve out more time for research. A professor of literature praised undergraduates who delayed finishing the term to pursue a complicated research assignment. "I give them incompletes if they need it. I have two students who are still working on this [project]. Good for them." This quotation exemplifies an unequivocal liberal view of education, which places idealistic goals (in this case, the completion of a well-researched paper) ahead of pragmatic goals. In this instance, a busy student may have to delay graduation and the means of acquiring a higher-paying job to satisfy the professor's standards.

A number of faculty members delegated the task of saving students' time to academic librarians. They expected librarians to help student researchers in locating resources in the databases and on the shelves in what one librarian dubbed "concierge-type information delivery." The professor in the following quotation demonstrated a preference for this model.

> I think librarians—[in] my experience personally and [in] the experience of students I've spoken to—librarians have a hard time figuring out separating themselves from their expertise and translating what they've found into something that the person inquiring needs and what I mean by that is overkill. All too often librarians give people more information than they actually need to be able to answer the questions that they have. And that's frustrating because sometimes people are simply looking for a small set of numbers or a specific source and librarians tend to offer much more than what they're being asked.

The faculty member suggested that librarians' subject matter expertise in research prevents them from taking simple requests at face value, thereby wasting patrons' time.

Librarians seemed to accept their role as time-savers, even if that role sometimes conflicted with their liberal ideals. One participant went so far as to say that "saving them time" was the most important thing librarians could do to ensure students' success. According to another colleague, the librarian has a *commitment* to respond to the needs of time-pressed students.

> ANTHROPOLOGIST: The amount of time that the student has to do his project changes the way you're going to help them significantly, it sounds like.
>
> LIBRARIAN: It does indeed. And I, I do have the commitment to say, "What is your immediate need? I'm gonna do my best to meet that immediate need." And in any small way to also provide skills that they can use independently in the future.

Here the participant defines two important functions of academic librarians. On the one hand, librarians must prepare students to become *independent* researchers, though such preparation is a time-consuming process that some students resist. On the other hand, as service professionals, librarians must respond to students' *immediate* needs.

"I'm a Little Nervous about Sort of Handing It to Them on a Silver Platter"

> [The librarian] actually has for a 300-level course of mine made up a wonderful web page with lots of resources available to [the students], which is good. I mean, I'm a little nervous about, you know, sort of handing it to them on a silver platter, but the task that they were asked to do was so challenging that in this case I thought it was, [laughs] it was very appropriate to really get them halfway there already in, in finding the archives out there.

Even as some faculty members expressed a desire for concierge-style information-delivery, others expressed ambivalence about the librarian's role as student time-saver. They questioned whether librarians prepare students to fulfill the idealistic mission of education through independent research or whether they enable vocational-minded students to skate by with minimal effort. The professor in the quotation above made a significant choice of metaphors. By using the idiom *to hand on a silver platter*, the faculty member implies that the librarian's assistance promotes student passivity, undermining both the pragmatic and idealistic purposes of education.

The idea that good research must be difficult was a recurrent theme in ERIAL interviews. Librarians like the one in the following quotation reinforced this view when discussing the complexity of today's information environment. "Increasingly our role is trying to educate people to the idea that there is no perfect search and you can't fulfill all your needs through one search box. It's not a one-stop shop when it comes to finding information. You've actually got to make a little effort." Professors used expressions like *challenging, rigorous,* and *pushing students* to describe their assignments. In response to the question of how to ensure students' success, a professor of Latin American Studies said,

You develop a good rapport with them and you challenge them intellectually. That's what they're here for, that's what they want even though they might not say it, but that's what they, you know, when you graduate from high school and you say, "I'm going to college. I'm gonna really be doing intellectually challenging work."

Although studies and surveys indicate that the majority of university students have a pragmatic view of education, the participant projects idealistic values on them. "That's what they're here for, even though they might not say it."

Interestingly, faculty interviews exposed hints of severity tied to idealist values. A professor of biology said, "My own personal preference would be that students aren't guided to everything. They are given the tools to get going, and then the students are expected to struggle a little if they have to struggle to get to where they need to get to." A professor of English agreed, "It's really important for every researcher to experience nothing . . . When [the students] did discover [an appropriate research topic] and they were passionate about, and that sense of discovery was made all the better, I guess, for their having endured, you know, the sufferings of a primary researcher." Consequently, discomfort and inconvenience are key ingredients to learning.

CONCLUSIONS AND RECOMMENDATIONS

This study of the influence of pragmatism and idealism on faculty members and librarians reveals several major findings. First, idealistic faculty members were conflicted about how to serve their pragmatic students. Unlike students who might measure success with grades or degree completion, faculty defined student success in terms of growth and the completion of an interesting, thoroughly researched assignment. In general, professors sympathized with today's overworked and overextended students. However, at times they still attributed student pragmatism to a lack of intellectual curiosity or a resistance to new ideas. Hence, faculty members felt a responsibility to push their students intellectually with rigorous research assignments. If faculty members have been making concessions to their time-pressed students, those concessions did not appear in this study. ERIAL professors instead sought ways to inspire students to give more time to their research.

ERIAL librarians were also conflicted about how best to serve students. They shared faculty members' understanding of the liberal-progressive mission of higher education, along with the wish that students would demonstrate more persistence and passion for the research process. They likewise shared in faculty's sympathy for overextended students. Unlike the faculty, though, librarians saw themselves in the dual roles of educators and service professionals. As service professionals, they tried to meet students' immediate needs, even if that sometimes meant delivering information rather than teaching information literacy skills.

It was precisely librarians' role as helpers that complicated their relationship with faculty. Some professors felt that the patron should dictate the amount of help a librarian provided in the style of a "concierge" information-delivery service. Others seemed uncomfortable with referring students to librarians for assistance. This was not because of any problem with *librarians,* but rather a problem with the concept of research *assistance.* In the liberal model of higher education, in which knowledge is its own reward, professors expect students to struggle. The struggle sweetens the experience of discovery. Librarians who aid time-pressed student procrastinators, or even hard-working and idealistic students, undermine this model.

I believe this study has value in raising librarian awareness of the tensions and contradictions around views of the research process, and as a result, I have a number of recommendations to make based on my conclusions.

I would begin by suggesting that we academic librarians should question ourselves about our personal beliefs regarding the purpose of higher education. Do we fully embrace both the liberal and pragmatic missions of the university? If we quietly hope to convert all students to the liberal ideals of higher education, we may miss opportunities to connect with a pragmatic student body. Before we can inspire students to research with enthusiasm and passion, we must present ourselves as professionals with a valuable service to provide. By financial necessity, many of today's students have limited time to devote to their research.

Now more than ever, academic librarians should seek to "save the time of the reader."[2] Following this principle entails both simple and complex changes in the way we think and talk about our services. We might take a page from tutoring centers, for example, and advertise our reference desk as "Research Help. *Walk-ins welcome.*" We might also empower our students to set the length of the reference interview by creating separate queues for "quick questions," in retail fashion. Some universities have already met with success by expanding reference services during finals. The library might create special online and print learning aids for student procrastinators at the middle and end of the term, highlighting the chat box, full-text features, online tutorials, and drop-in services. And instruction sessions could always highlight one time-saving tip, like the full-text limiter on databases.

It is a more difficult task, perhaps, to change the research models and values of those faculty members who distrust all librarian interventions. The best remedy for this issue may be to redouble our outreach efforts to current graduate students. In that way, the professors of tomorrow will have positive models of librarian-student interactions. They will come to value the different levels of librarian assistance and see that our work, while helpful to the time-pressed student, need not reduce the student to a passive recipient of information. Also, if we are not already doing so, we might work harder to assist faculty members in their own research, thereby establishing a model of cooperative research.

I propose various areas of further study to deepen our understanding of pragmatism and idealism in the academic library. This chapter examined interviews from faculty and librarians at two institutions. It would be ideal to expand this analysis to the other three institutions involved in the ERIAL project and to break down faculty responses by discipline. Student interviews might also play part of an expanded study, since faculty and librarians could discuss only their perceptions of student values and experiences. It would be especially revealing to look at student descriptions of struggle in their research, to confirm or challenge faculty perceptions on the role of discomfort in education. Finally, in a number of ERIAL interviews, librarian participants discussed the importance of providing busy, pragmatic students with nonjudgmental service. I would like to see a study measuring how well we are accomplishing that task.

NOTES

1. Common criteria of a good research paper included (1) a strong thesis statement, hypothesis, or topic; (2) interesting subject matter or writer enthusiasm; (3) comprehensiveness, rigor, or depth; (4) demonstration of proper writing mechanics; (5) inclusion of scholarly or authoritative resources; (6) appropriate number of resources for the scope of the project; (7) resource variety; and (8) correct use of citations.

2. The concept that librarians must save the time of the reader first appeared as the fourth law of Ranganathan's 1963 *The Five Laws of Library Science.*

3

Marketing the Library's Instructional Services to Teaching Faculty: Learning from Teaching Faculty Interviews

ANNIE ARMSTRONG

While many faculty members value their experiences with traditional course-integrated instruction, either in the form of class visits to the library or in-class presentations delivered by librarians, many others view teaching research skills as their own domain and devote time both within and outside of classroom hours to teaching the same research skills which librarians aim to impart in library instruction sessions. Some faculty teach research skills because they view this as their natural role, while others may not be aware of the library instruction options available on their campus, or may not find it feasible to reserve classroom teaching hours for library instruction sessions. Others enjoy a combination of both iterations: teaching research skills to their students and calling upon the expertise of librarians to expand upon research concepts taught in class.

Other instructors express hesitancy to collaborate with librarians due to uneven experiences with the library or perceived limitations in instructional services available to them. Taking into account the lack of consensus among faculty as to who should teach research skills and how this teaching might occur, the goals of this chapter are twofold: to provide insights into the modes of instructional services to which faculty might respond positively, and to offer insights into communication and marketing strategies that could increase faculty buy-in to library instruction in support of student learning.

Interviews of teaching faculty administered by the two anthropologists for the ERIAL Project revealed widespread and often dissenting viewpoints about the need for, desired outcomes of, and format of instructional services offered by the library. The wide range of instructional services sought, and the varying modes in which these services might be delivered, suggest that, in addition to—or perhaps in preparation for—marketing library instruction to teaching faculty, librarians need to conceive of a suite of instructional services flexible enough to meet the diverse teaching styles and needs of faculty.

THE IMPORTANCE OF LIBRARY INSTRUCTION IN HIGHER EDUCATION

In their seminal text, *Information Literacy: Theory and Practice,* Esther Grassian and Joan Kaplowitz contend that library instruction should be incorporated into the mission of academic, school, public, and special libraries alike, as "advances in information technology and the proliferation of information in both print and electronic formats have created an even more pressing need to develop an information literate society" (2009, 267). Grassian and Kaplowitz detail historical developments in the information literacy instruction movement and provide a thorough review of the information literacy literature, including pedagogy, assessment, and instructional design. While numerous studies investigate the impact of library instruction on student research skills, a high proportion of these are case studies which examine relatively small user populations at individual universities and don't effectively speak to the value of library instruction on a larger scale.

Larger-scale studies such as "The Value of Academic Libraries Project" by the Association of College and Research Libraries are emerging to study the impact of academic libraries on the national level, addressing issues such as the effects of various library services on student retention and student attitudes about the university (Hinchliffe and Oakleaf 2010). "Project Information Literacy," another national study currently under way, investigates the research habits of college students throughout the United States, examining "how information literacy training and coaching is provided to early adults by professors and librarians for conducting course-related research and for 'everyday life' research" (http://projectin folit.org). Clearly, large-scale studies are emerging to explore student research skills and demonstrate the impact of libraries on students' information literacy skills. The ERIAL Project offers a unique perspective on the relationship between student research skills and the role of the library by producing qualitative data from ethnographic interviews of three groups of stakeholders involved in the student research process: students, librarians, and faculty.

SCOPE AND METHODOLOGY

The insights offered in this chapter incorporate and synthesize faculty perspectives on student research behavior and learning needs, as well as faculty expectations of library instruction and support as expressed in faculty interviews administered by the ERIAL Project's two anthropologists. Seventy-five faculty interviews were conducted at the five ERIAL universities. Analysis provided in this chapter does not provide a comparison of faculty perspectives at different institutions, nor does it emphasize faculty opinions specific to subject disciplines or the academic level of students taught (e.g. first-year, upperclassmen, or graduate students). Rather, faculty comments have been thematically grouped and stripped of institution-specific information. The rationale behind this decision is to provide a holistic view of faculty insights regarding student research needs and how these needs ought to be addressed. Furthermore, this choice was made so that the insights gained from interviews could apply to a diverse audience of librarians, from those at small private colleges to those at large public universities.

PERCEPTIONS OF STUDENT NEED FOR RESEARCH INSTRUCTION: A BRIEF SUMMARY

While faculty interviews provided voluminous data pertaining to specific research skills students need in order to successfully complete research assignments, this chapter places more focus on exploring potential models for how research skills might be taught and supported. Faculty recognized that many students have deficits in their knowledge and skills relating to the research process. Faculty often referred to the following areas of weakness: finding appropriate research tools beyond Google and Wikipedia, understanding the overall purpose of the library, navigating the library to find materials, assessing the quality and reliability of information, discerning between different types of materials (popular magazines versus peer-reviewed journals), conducting effective keyword searches, narrowing topics, citing sources, and avoiding plagiarism.

Faculty often commented on student research behaviors they perceived as deficient. One English professor stated that students "really need to be reintroduced to what a library does. How it is built and how it is situated and where the stacks are and what a Dewey Decimal System is and what a Library of Congress system is." A faculty member in history remarked, "[Students'] first instinct is to search the Internet. Google. And it's not that there aren't good and valuable things to be gotten there, but they're not trained to differentiate." Similarly, a faculty member in foreign languages and literatures remarked that students are "not aware of the difference between a good source, a mediocre source, and a terrible source. To them they're all the same." These comments are representative of a belief held by many faculty that students arrive at college with an inability to discern between various types of sources and identify reliable and high-quality research materials. Furthermore, many students lack knowledge about where to search for quality research materials.

In general, the skills faculty members believed students need to become savvy researchers and the skills that librarians teach in library instruction sessions align closely with the ACRL's Objectives for Information Literacy Instruction (Association of College and Research Libraries 2001). However, many faculty comments indicated that librarians may need to address more basic instructional outcomes than previously assumed; a library instruction session to first-year students which begins with teaching students to navigate the library website to find articles and books may fail to address the more fundamental needs of students who lack knowledge about the overall purpose of the library and the materials it contains. Librarians might do well to take a step back and imagine student needs not only as they pertain to navigating the virtual world, but also as they relate to navigating the physical world of the library's reference area and book stacks. Perhaps offering general orientations and tours would help to meet the needs of students who lack basic familiarity with navigating the academic library, as well as providing a conceptual basis for the organization of information.

FACULTY IMPRESSIONS ABOUT WHERE RESEARCH SHOULD BE TAUGHT

Interviews with teaching faculty revealed that a great amount of overlap occurs between research skills taught by faculty and research skills taught by librarians. Faculty often view teaching research skills as their domain, and may call upon librarians only to supplement the research instruction they provide throughout the semester. This overlap can offer insights into how librarians might market instructional services and conceive of instructional models that align with faculty teaching preferences.

Faculty interviews revealed that faculty address myriad research skills within the classroom and while meeting with students during office hours or at the library. Faculty teach research skills including, but not limited to, how to narrow topics, develop effective keyword searches, search library catalogs and article indexes, use interlibrary loan, evaluate sources, and correctly cite sources. Many faculty comments depicted scenarios of faculty working with students to help them with research. A professor in educational leadership mentioned that she provides students with a library instruction sheet and that she "take[s] them [students] from the home page and show[s] them how to find articles, how to find books, how to order books, how to get books delivered, then how to find dissertations." A faculty member in comparative religion stated that he physically brings students to the library where the librarians "show [the students] the reference section, go up to the fourth level [main collection] section, and encourage them to check out at least a couple of books for their research papers." Some faculty instructed students on how to effectively search electronic resources. A professor in communications noted: "[Students] don't understand search and how to use specific keywords and how those keywords might be different from database to database, so those are the kinds of things that I feel that I need to prep them with before they do their research."

Remarks from faculty about helping students to navigate various aspects of the research process could indicate both a willingness to teach research skills and a sense of responsibility to do so. Whatever reasons faculty may have for teaching these skills (some of which will be explored later in this chapter), the fact that they choose to do so suggests that librarians could provide instructional materials to augment the teaching that takes place in the classroom. For example, librarians could create print and electronic guides providing instruction in conducting research on various subjects. This sort of help would allow librarians to support faculty with research instruction without "taking it away" from them, simultaneously providing a channel through which to communicate accurate and up-to-date information about the research process and library tools.

Furthermore, since many faculty described scenarios in which they worked one-on-one with students during office hours, librarians might be able to gain an entrée into collaborating with faculty by providing and advertising their own "office hours," or "consultation" hours, in addition to the hours in which they are available at the reference desk. In marketing such services, adopting teaching faculty terminology (using terms such as "office hours" or "consultation hours" rather than library-based terminology) might help teaching faculty and students to understand that librarians are available to provide individualized research assistance.

FACULTY REFLECTIONS ABOUT ENLISTING THE HELP OF LIBRARIANS

Faculty interviews abounded with reflections about the value of the work that librarians do with students, and the positive aspects of collaborating with librarians to provide library instruction and one-on-one research help to students. A cognitive psychology professor exalted "the value of having the librarian teach the students how to use the search engine. How to use the thesaurus and PsycINFO to find the right keywords, for example." An English professor also explained that "defining a search, working on a topic is part of the process," going on to state that "librarians can help students with that part of the research process by taking the time to say 'what do you mean by that?' So students do get the chance to run at that point in the process, a rough version but a version of their argument by someone, and that's really helpful." A vocal performance faculty member lauded the value of teaching with librarians, remarking, "I like the way we teach my class. I'm always present when she's presenting so that I could say, 'by the way, I want you to have this many references for this paper, or by the way you should read this many abstracts,' because she doesn't necessarily know the content area or she might not even know what keywords to suggest. So I think teaching together has been very useful. She's primarily teaching but I chime in as I think of things." Moreover, another faculty member spoke of the librarian's role in helping students find information and acting as "the wind in their sails," going on to state that "teaching them specific things and teaching them how to judge a source is all beautiful and everything but I think there is a really important human aspect to what the librarians do that is crucial to helping students."

These comments, and similar testimonials, could be leveraged as selling points for both library instruction and the overall value of working directly with librarians. Faculty frequently described the librarian's role as that of a mediator, complimentary voice, or expert. Faculty expected librarians to project a knowledgeable, encouraging, and approachable demeanor to students who are often overwhelmed and occasionally discouraged by the tasks involved with the research process. The positive remarks of faculty who valued instruction suggest that in devising effective marketing messages to convince more reluctant faculty to take advantage of instructional services, librarians should emphasize their role not only as experts in research, but as mentors and encouragers of students, both within and outside of the classroom.

In order to effectively "sell" this image to all faculty, librarians as a group must consistently project an upbeat and encouraging demeanor. A few faculty members described ways in which librarians project an off-putting public image. For instance, one faculty member remarked that "all too often librarians give people more information than they actually need to be able to answer the questions that they have." Another professor stated:

"I think they need to be aware that students find them intimidating, that it's very hard if a librarian's on the phone or typing on their computer, to try and go and interrupt somebody that you look at as being an authority figure, because they do see librarians as authority figures, and so it's really important for librarians to be open and accessible, and just be conscious of that." An anthropology professor emphasized the importance of giving students a positive message: "So often I have students who leave the library feeling discouraged . . . And even if they have, you know a really horrible time trying to find something, you know, they should be sent back with a positive message saying, 'well, now that you know it's not there, how can you think of ways of reconfiguring your research that will work with some of the sources we have?' Students don't always leave with that kind of upbeat message."

At times, faculty saw librarians as intimidating students through their behavior, and as either overwhelming students by bombarding them with more information than they could digest, or discouraging them by sending them away from the library empty-handed. Librarians need to develop and project consistent standards regarding service and instruction. Gauging how much information a particular student might need, or suggesting alternative sources as necessary are important skills that librarians need to maintain and sharpen throughout their careers (see also chapter 2).

FACULTY SUGGESTIONS FOR ENHANCING LIBRARY INSTRUCTION

During interviews, teaching faculty often remarked about potential improvements to library instruction. Some of these remarks suggested a desire for a more communicative and collaborative relationship in general, while others were more specific, pointing to services librarians could provide to augment their existing instructional offerings.

Some teaching faculty sought to arrange for a librarian to work with their students throughout the semester so that the librarian could establish a better rapport with students and provide help on an ongoing basis. Faculty comments suggested that librarians might be able to strengthen their connections to faculty by marketing options for more sustained interactions with a class. For example, a faculty member in English remarked that it might be useful to "partner with a librarian," adding that it might benefit students to "see the librarian more regularly in some way." One faculty member even sought to arrange six classroom visits from a librarian throughout the semester in order for the librarian to build a rapport with students, explaining that "rapport is a key part to making the students want to be more active."

Some faculty believed that students should learn the overall purpose of the library early on in their college careers as a part of the orientation process, or at least during their first year, and not necessarily as a part of a specific course. Furthermore, in addition to—or perhaps prior to—learning how to search databases and catalogs and find and evaluate resources, students need a more basic education grounding them in the purpose of libraries, and academic libraries in particular. Faculty comments suggested that attempts to market instruction should not be confined to a course-integrated scenario. For instance, one history professor speculated, "I don't know, is there anything incorporated into the orientation of new students to help familiarize themselves . . . to most effectively utilize resources in the library, something like that would be really good." Another historian expressed her beliefs about what students know about libraries in contrast to what they ought to know:

> I think they should learn what a library is early, before they have ma-
> jors. And I'm not kidding about what a library is because I think most
> of them have not spent any time in libraries as children, whereas my
> generation, we went to the library as kids. I don't know how many
> of the students I see actually know what a library is and would have
> ever borrowed a book from a public library. So that their, their whole
> notion of where information resides, what types of books there are,
> that there are different types of books . . . They really need a lot more
> education about that. And they need to be educated about it in a way
> that is revelatory for them.

In addition to pursuing collaborative relationships with faculty in academic departments, faculty comments suggested that librarians should also focus their energies on inserting themselves and the library into the general orientation process on their campuses, finding a memorable and "revelatory" way to persuade students about the importance of the library early on in their academic careers.

Librarians often observed that students seemed to respond best to instruction provided at the time of need. Teaching faculty often expressed a willingness to integrate instructional content into their courses to reinforce the outcomes of a library instruction session. Whether supplemental instructional materials take the form of print handouts, online tutorials, or course research guides, enlisting the cooperation of teaching faculty in integrating supplementary materials to facilitate the review of key research concepts would send the message that librarians are interested in going beyond the confines of a single library instruction session. These tools would likely be useful to a broader base of teaching faculty who may not opt to schedule a library instruction session. Faculty described multiple types of instructional materials that they would find helpful for their teaching. One faculty member in English expressed a desire for "more canned teaching modules designed to guide students through learning how to use MLA bibliography," to "augment the face-to-face teaching that we have." Similarly, a professor suggested that librarians "give them clear directions . . . as to how to use the databases," requesting that librarians provide these directions as both a handout and online in the form of "snippets or video clips, and so on." This faculty member suggested that such supplementary instructional aids would help students "because they tend to forget, especially if they already feel overwhelmed by a specific subject."

BARRIERS TO SUCCESSFUL COLLABORATIONS: IMPLICATIONS FOR REACHING THE RESISTANT OR THE UNAWARE

Interviews with teaching faculty revealed several barriers to scheduling library instruction sessions and collaborating with librarians, including the poor outcomes or quality of past experiences, lack of awareness of the available options or how to go about taking advantage of them, and time. By acknowledging these impediments and exploring remedies to alleviate them, librarians may be able to provide faculty with more workable options for incorporating library instruction into their courses.

As expected, numerous teaching faculty named "time" as a major factor limiting their ability to work with librarians. This barrier could translate as not wanting to give up valuable class time for a library instruction session or not finding time to collaborate with a librarian. For instance, one faculty member remarked, "I really like having the librarian come in, but I don't do it for every class. It is only where I think it is really necessary. Because we have a limited number of sessions, and it takes one of the sessions." Likewise, another faculty member mentioned that "the hardest thing to manage is that you do get really busy in the semester and that weighs on the sort of interactions you can have with the librarians. If we had more time to meet and discuss and build out the interaction, that would be great. But the frustrating thing is that you get so busy, that that's hard to do."

Many faculty said that they could not conceive of a way to carve out valuable class time to devote to an instruction session. Librarians might be able to leverage testimonials from other teaching faculty who have experienced the time-saving merits of working with librarians to decrease the amount of time spent teaching research skills both in class and outside of classroom hours. Additionally, reducing the burden involved with setting up instruction by making it clear and easy who to contact and simplifying scheduling procedures could sway busy faculty. As one communication professor said, "Ideally, I'd like to be able to call somebody, have my contact person or my point person, I'd like to be able to call somebody and say 'this is the project I'm assigning, what do you think we could do to make this a better process for the kids?'. . . But I'd like to know who to call in the first place, and I think that's the biggest hurdle." If librarians routinely contacted faculty to advertise and schedule instruction rather than placing the onus on the faculty to do so, they might be able to convince more faculty to incorporate instruction into their courses.

While many faculty viewed library instruction as a useful enhancement to their own teaching, there were some who expressed negative perceptions of the value of instruction based on prior experiences. One English professor claimed that "there's no way to make the actual process of library instruction interesting. Some are better than others, but it's boring. It becomes interesting when there is actually something specific of one's own that's invested in it." He continued, noting that he "would like to find a way to incorporate library instruction that was detailed enough to really actually cover stuff. But have it fit into a class in a way that students actually learn as opposed to just zoning out." Another English faculty member provided the following criticism of library instruction: "I don't know if there's always a strong transfer in terms of their skills. And it's not the fault of the librarian; it's just where they are and how they are at that moment. So I haven't found the ideal moment to bring [students] to the library and have an orientation for something in particular. I've also found that there's some unevenness in terms of how the [library] presentations work."

The above remarks allude to multiple characteristics of library instruction detracting from its usefulness. Given the fact that many faculty members are reluctant to devote class time to an instruction session, librarians need to do what they can to ensure that library instruction is both engaging and worthwhile. Although teaching styles obviously vary from one librarian to the next, guidelines should exist to ensure that learning outcomes for commonly taught courses and workshops remain consistent. Training for librarians and peer-evaluation procedures should also be in place to increase consistency and ensure quality from one librarian to the next. Additionally, librarians who incorporate active learning exercises, discussion, and ample hands-on research time into library instruction sessions may have more success in capturing the attention of students. Given the fact that some faculty may view instruction as a tedious experience for students to endure, librarians may be able to increase faculty buy-in by advertising a flexible menu of instructional offerings. For instance, rather than vaguely describing library instruction on the library website or a brochure, librarians could describe specific models from which faculty could choose. Instead of scheduling a "standard" library instruction session in which the librarian teaches for an hour, faculty could opt to schedule an hour of mediated hands-on research time preceded by a very brief introduction to one or two research tools.

By advertising examples of flexible instructional options to faculty through a variety of communication channels (e.g. via e-mail, presentations, meetings, or brochures), librarians might be able to spread the message that instruction can be tailored to specific faculty needs. While some faculty may prefer to place most decisions in the hands of librarians, others may respond more positively to having more of a voice in determining what content is covered, and how.

THE FACULTY DEMAND FOR INCREASED OUTREACH AND COMMUNICATION

In discussing the library, a management faculty member remarked, "I think it's an underutilized resource and probably largely because people don't know all the things that can be done. And so, that's what I'm saying. I think more outreach is necessary." Faculty comments regarding how they prefer to receive information about the library can be divided into four categories: electronic, print-based, face-to-face, and liaison relationships. The common denominator underlying these categories is the overarching desire of faculty to receive updated information from the library. By broadcasting marketing messages through a variety of channels on a regular basis, librarians might be able to increase faculty knowledge of library services, thereby increasing the chances that faculty will take advantage of services they did not know existed.

Many teaching faculty indicated a desire to receive more information electronically. While harnessing the power of Web 2.0 technologies in an attempt to increase awareness of library services in the online environment is likely not a new idea to most librarians, many faculty comments suggested that such efforts need to be increased. One history professor remarked, "I'd love to get regular updates about new things, new databases, new features, you know I'd love to have like a little RSS thing from the library." A business professor similarly asked, "So how do librarians show their visibility in an electronic environment? So how can they tell me what to look out at the latest collection, for example? Rather than sending a global e-mail. So how can they engage individually? I think they have the capacity through electronic means to do that. So they should leverage and exploit the new technologies that they have access to." For example, a communications professor responded positively to a librarian who utilized Facebook to connect with students, explaining that "she had a Facebook presence to communicate with students, and also to communicate with colleagues and let us know about new features the library was offering, and new services that were available." A kinesiology faculty member observed that the library website "could do a better job of promoting the library's value," going on to state that "it [the website] provides a service to the community, but it's also a marketing and self-promotion tool. And actually there is one thing that I would like to see more of here. I'd like to see some classes run out of the library. I'd like to see workshops around here. I'd like to see authors come and do book signings here. I'd like to see some buzz about it's cool to learn in a library."

Whether comments regarding electronic communication are general or specific, they share a common message: the library's efforts to leverage technologies in order to increase awareness of library services do not always achieve the desired impact. Attempts to market the library's value via the website should be accompanied by other activities and services such as workshops, classes, author signings, and any activities that would generate a "buzz," convincing the campus community that the library is a lively locus of intellectual activity.

Some faculty referred to more traditional marketing methods that they would respond positively to. For instance, one faculty member suggested that "if there were more posters around campus, more e-mails going out, or if they gave out calendars. I think they give out bookmarks . . . Anything that they could do to make their services available to students would be a good thing." An English professor member simply stated, "Just send us brochures." These requests for traditional marketing materials emphasize the need for the library to market itself through a variety of media in order to reach a broad audience.

LIAISON RELATIONSHIPS AND FACE-TO-FACE COMMUNICATION

Comments in which faculty expressed a desire to work with a specific point person or liaison suggest that they might respond more positively to the option of working with a specific librarian than they would to more anonymous models such as going to the library website and scheduling instruction through a general form which is then sent to an unknown source. Faculty members' discussions relating to liaison relationships suggested that providing faculty with the name and contact information of a specific person (likely in the form of a departmental library liaison) might simplify and personalize the process of arranging for library instruction to a degree that might significantly increase faculty participation in library instruction. A communications faculty member described an "ideal scenario" as "having a person, dedicated again, to a discipline, having that person interact frequently with a class, so definitely having them come to class to introduce the library, and then creating opportunities for subsequent interaction and help as the students progress and work on their project." An educational leadership faculty member also referenced library liaisons in her "ideal scenario" of working with librarians: "the library was fully staffed and the liaison from the library to each individual department had time then to spend in that department. Even if that was an hour a week, something where that librarian was available to talk with faculty and to exchange ideas and have some face-to-face conversations." Another faculty member described working with a library liaison, saying "[I] always give my students [the librarian's] name and . . . explain to them that she's available plus that there's always a reference librarian of some sort available that will actually sit down and meet with them. So, I tell them that . . . they're always shocked to hear that someone will sit down and meet with them."

Liaison relationships provide teaching faculty the opportunity to build partnerships with librarians over time. This system might also cut down on faculty time often involved in setting up instruction. In addition to their potential for streamlining the process of arranging library instruction sessions, liaison relationships allow librarians to provide faculty with updated information about library research tools and services that faculty may use in their own research and/or work with students.

While some faculty voiced an interest in working with a library liaison, others expressed a general desire for increased face-to-face communication with librarians, mentioning numerous scenarios in which this communication might occur. Faculty offered several suggestions as to how librarians could increase their visibility by making a more concerted effort to participate in (or initiate) meetings with faculty. For example, one biology professor stated that "there should be more communication than there is. Like, actually set meetings maybe once a semester where librarians come over and meet or faculty goes over there and it's like a required meeting . . . because every department has different needs from the library and those needs get specifically addressed." Another faculty member provided the following suggestion: "Get six librarians in a room with six first-year writing program teachers. And hashing out ideas, making suggestions. 'Cause when you put a lot of people together I think the ideas start hopping." A kinesiology faculty member extolled the value of relationships, stating that "people need relationships, they need face time, they need people to get out there from the library and promote the library. And there's a lot of quality here, it needs to be championed and you do that face-to-face, right?" They went on to suggest that the library offer "a program of support . . . I'm not saying it has to be really creative, it doesn't. But having that and having one or two key relationships on a very small scale on different colleges around the campus."

These comments indicate a willingness on the part of teaching faculty to meet with librarians in order to engage in discussions that could potentially build and improve upon collaborative relationships between librarians and teaching faculty. Every library can facilitate group discussions and/or departmental meetings with faculty in order to discuss key issues relating to teaching and research. Some faculty suggested that they would be receptive to new faculty library orientation. For example, one biology faculty member stated, "I, until recently, wasn't . . . familiar with their resources. So, maybe on that note, I don't know if this is something that's offered, but kind of an introduction to the library for new faculty members." A communications professor also admitted her unfamiliarity with the library's services: "Having an introduction to the library as a new instructor here would have been a nice—it would just be a nice way for me to find out what the different services are. I find—I feel that it's hard to find out all the things they have to offer."

These comments suggest that just as many faculty would like the library to take on a greater role in the student orientation process, they see a need for the library to provide a basic orientation to new faculty. By systematically seeking out new faculty, librarians could increase awareness of available instructional services and library resources, simultaneously projecting a welcoming image and establishing new relationships with faculty who have few preconceived notions about the library.

Several faculty provided comments suggesting that the library expand its efforts to support faculty with their own research pursuits. For instance, the communications faculty member above stated that "the graduate students and the new faculty are the people that really need the library's help, they're the ones that are publishing and writing and there's a lot of ways the library could meet the needs of that group." An anthropology professor also remarked, "I would love it if I knew that they were here for the faculty as well as the students and not just in a sense of helping the faculty help the students. But in helping the faculty directly would be great." Likewise, a writing professor observed that she enjoyed "the professional exchanges we can have about things."

In addition to offering a wide range of services in support of the educational mission of the university, librarians—even those who identify as instruction librarians—need to channel an equal level of support directly toward supporting faculty research. The research and publishing demands placed upon graduate students and teaching faculty require them to stay up-to-date with myriad technologies and research tools. Thus, in addition to approaching faculty in the name of helping students, librarians might have equal luck in forming relationships with faculty by increasing their efforts to update and inform faculty about useful resources for their own research and publishing endeavors. By convincing the faculty that they are knowledgeable about all areas of their work—above and beyond the realm of the classroom—librarians can only improve the image of the library on campus and increase the chances that faculty will take advantage of additional services such as library instruction.

CONCLUSION

The wide range of faculty views regarding library instruction and services suggests that there is no single method of marketing instructional services to teaching faculty to increase buy-in to library instruction. Teaching faculty harbor varying opinions as to how, and if, library instruction should be delivered, thus complicating the task of marketing this service. While some faculty might wish to schedule one or two library instruction sessions, others might prefer to schedule a full semester of visits and research consultations with a librarian. As librarians seek to increase faculty buy-in of library instruction, there is no single action, or a linear series of steps, that they could take that would meet the needs and communication styles of all teaching faculty simultaneously. Rather, librarians are faced with the considerable challenge of branching out in numerous directions to cater to the diverse needs and preferences of the greatest number of teaching faculty.

Once librarians imagine and design a suite of instructional services robust and flexible enough to coalesce with the diverse teaching needs of the faculty at their institutions, librarians can begin increasing awareness and buy-in to instruction by launching a systematic and continuous marketing campaign which leverages print, electronic, and interpersonal marketing methods. Libraries' marketing campaigns should be sustained, varied, and advertise a well-rounded menu of services. As evidenced by faculty interviews, the formation of informal professional relationships between librarians and teaching faculty could have equal if not greater impact on faculty willingness to partake in the library's instructional services than any number of marketing strategies. The information regarding instruction and marketing gleaned from faculty interviews clearly reflects that every effort to offer and publicize services and establish and strengthen professional relationships has the potential to appeal to a different faculty niche.

4

Why Don't Students Ask Librarians for Help? Undergraduate Help-Seeking Behavior in Three Academic Libraries

SUSAN MILLER AND NANCY MURILLO

L ibrarians can offer crucial assistance to undergraduate students doing academic research. These information professionals teach students how to access information, advising students on the most up-to-date search techniques and sources, as well as how to evaluate information. Many times, students do not know exactly what information they are seeking as they conduct their research, and librarians can play a critical role in helping students define their information needs and learn how to sort out the welter of sources available. By teaching students how to conceptualize the research process, librarians can help students explore and define their research interests. Furthermore, because they work at the physical and virtual sites where students are doing research (i.e., the physical library and its Web presence), librarians are uniquely placed to offer these services, helping students articulate and meet their needs when students are most in need of those types of help.

However, students do not necessarily ask librarians for help. Library literature suggests that students have a limited understanding of what librarians can do for them (e.g., Swope and Katzer 1972; Burns and Harper 2007). This literature also suggests that instead of going to librarians for help, students seek assistance from professors, friends, and others (e.g., Robinson and Reid 2007; Vondracek 2007).[1]

In this chapter, we take the analysis of the help-seeking process a step further, identifying characteristics of relationships inside and outside the library that influence students to seek some individuals for help rather than others. We ask: Do students seek help from people other than librarians, and why do students go to these individuals? How do these relationships affect students' relationships with librarians, and when students get help, is that assistance beneficial? To answer these questions, we briefly review selected literature from library studies on student help-seeking, and suggest how its focus can be extended to include how the dynamics of students' relationships with professors, peers, and family affect whether students will seek them out for help. We also describe how students' relationships are influenced by their connections with universities, neighborhoods, and information sources. We explore how these themes are present in the ethnographic data from the ERIAL Project, as well as reasons why some students do not seek help from anyone. Based upon these data, we also propose some ways in which librarians may improve services for students.

STUDENT HELP-SEEKING BEHAVIOR AND STUDENTS' RELATIONSHIPS

The library literature on student help-seeking tends to focus on identifying the types of individuals whom students seek for help and on characterizing students' experience and understanding of librarians and libraries. However, there has been less focus on why students seek particular helpers. We suggest how additional data on these relationships and the social contexts in which they occur might further explain why students go to people other than librarians.

Students often seek certain types of individuals for help, though there has been less exploration of why they do so. Recent works have suggested that students often prefer to seek help from peers or instructors (Robinson and Reid 2007; Vondracek 2007). In one study, students most frequently sought help from professors or teaching assistants, from friends and family somewhat less often, and from librarians and students who were not friends least frequently (Vondracek 2007). In another study, 67 percent of first-year biology students primarily went to friends for help (Callinan 2005). There has been less analysis of why students prefer particular helpers, though Vondracek (2007) notes that students may approach some people for help because students consider those individuals to be the persons most knowledgeable about their research topics.

Students' experiences with librarians and understanding of librarians' roles may also determine whether students seek help from them. Some students may not ask librarians for help because they do not want to be bothersome (Swope and Katzer 1972), or because they feel librarians would not necessarily want to help them (Ruppel and Fagan 2002). Some students may be unaware of the services that are available to them in the library (Robinson and Reid 2007), or of the educational roles of librarians (Swope and Katzer 1972; Burns and Harper 2007). And in some cases, students may be dissatisfied with past service at the library (Swope and Katzer 1972).

Often, the library literature references "library anxiety," first delineated by Constance Mellon in her 1986 landmark study (e.g., Sobel 2009; Robinson and Reid 2007). Library anxiety, a discomfort that students may feel in the academic library, can translate into a reluctance to seek help from librarians at the reference desk. For example, in their qualitative study of undergraduate students' help-seeking behavior, Robinson and Reid (2007) found that students who chose not to seek help from librarians expressed "symptoms" of library anxiety including feeling nervous or lost in the library.

Other studies identifying related themes of unease suggest that students may feel that their questions are too basic (Swope and Katzer 1972) or they may feel foolish for not knowing how to do library research (Ruppel and Fagan 2002).

We suggest that further exploration of the dynamics of students' relationships in and out of the library may broaden our understanding of how students seek help. Students' relationships may affect whom students perceive to be sources of help, and students' evaluation of how appropriate these helpers may be. Students' relationships may put some helpers in position not only to share information (and misinformation) about librarians but also to affect students' attitudes about librarians and whether students will ask librarians for help. By including these characteristics in our understanding of help-seeking, we will have a more comprehensive picture of the help-seeking process that will enable us to design services to help students more effectively.

DATA AND METHODS

Our analysis is based on 91 ethnographic interviews conducted with undergraduates and 45 ethnographic interviews with teaching faculty from Northeastern Illinois University, DePaul University, and the University of Illinois at Chicago. Data selected from student interviews included students' descriptions of when they had last sought help with academic research projects and of the last research projects they completed for class. Since interviews were semi-structured, students brought up help-seeking throughout the conversations; relevant sections of text were identified and coded. Sections of interviews were also identified in which students were not seeking help but could have been. Data selected from faculty interviews included text related to faculty members' perceptions of librarians' roles. Data were analyzed using a modified method of analysis described by Emerson, Fretz, and Shaw (1995). For further details of recruitment, data collection, and analysis methods, see chapter 1 of this volume.

RESULTS

We begin with a description of students' lack of relationships with librarians, contrasting this situation with the types of relationships students have with professors, peers, and family, and noting ways in which relationships with nonlibrarian helpers do not necessarily succeed in supporting students. We then describe how the institution of the university structures students' relationships with librarians, particularly via students' relationships with their professors. We detail how some students seek help from public librarians in their neighborhoods instead of academic librarians, and problems that students may have in their research as a result. Finally, we discuss reasons why some students do not seek help, preferring instead to be self-reliant, or being unaware that help is needed, and the research difficulties these students face.

Not Having Relationships with Librarians

Students may not go to librarians for help. When we asked students about their most recent experiences working with librarians on research projects, many students' responses indicated that, at best, these undergraduates had limited relationships with librarians: many of our student interviewees had never asked librarians for help or had only made simple requests of librarians. Furthermore, these students did not necessarily know what librarians could do. A number of students indicated that they were unsure which members of staff even were librarians.

When students do not have relationships with librarians, it may be in part because these students had little idea what librarians can do for them. A junior women's studies major who had never worked with a librarian said, "To be honest with you, I didn't understand how they could help me." A senior psychology major explained,

> I really don't know much of what exactly they [librarians] do . . . in terms of research. My idea is that they're there if I ask, "I can't find this book. Would you help me find it? Where's this aisle? Where would I find education things—is it [on the] second, third floor?" Kind of that way—directions more than anything else.

Like this student, a number of our participants said that they only expected librarians to be able to help with directions in the physical library. Students also tended to say only that they believed that librarians could assist them with finding books, particularly volumes that were known items. A junior elementary education major, for example, said the most significant way a librarian could help would be "just like . . . 'I'm looking for this book.' Maybe they can look it up sometimes for us, and just tell us where it is. I've never had or thought of any other situation where a librarian would help." These students are not merely declining librarians' help, they do not seem to know librarians are able to offer further assistance with research.

Another example of students' lack of awareness of librarians' role is the following conversation with a junior sociology major. As part of a photo journaling exercise, he photographed the first floor of his university's library, showing the reference and circulation desks. He was asked about getting help there:

ANTHROPOLOGIST: Would you say that on the right at that desk and on the left at that other desk there's different types of help available or would you say it's mostly the same people who do that kind of work?

STUDENT: I noticed that there's different signs there, something like that . . . but I didn't notice that until . . . I went to meet with you, otherwise I probably would have thought it was exactly the same thing. And . . . I still kind of think that they can help me with similar things. I don't see—why they couldn't.

ANTHROPOLOGIST: Let me ask you. One of those banners [above one of the desks] is marked "Circulation." What does that term mean to you?

STUDENT: As, in terms of like—a library circulation? I don't know. Maybe checking out books.

ANTHROPOLOGIST: And the other one over here is "Reference." What's that?

STUDENT: Reference? I don't know. Either you, I go there for help or I doubt it has anything to do with actually reference books. Maybe they're like a reference book. You go there and ask them all sorts of questions.

. . .

ANTHROPOLOGIST: What sorts of questions would you imagine you can ask at the reference desk?

STUDENT: Hmm, questions about where things might be.

ANTHROPOLOGIST: Anything else?

STUDENT: Hmm, any help. Just help generally with the library.

ANTHROPOLOGIST: What other kinds of help might you ask about?

STUDENT: I don't know.

As with some of our other participants, this student articulates that librarians can provide directional assistance. Additionally, he seems not to know the difference between librarians at the reference desk and staff at the circulation desk, a perception which in this case seems to be complicated by his unfamiliarity with the spaces in which library employees are working.

Certainly, some students we met expected and received more substantive help with research from librarians, including help identifying keywords, learning how to use the databases and catalog, and finding items when they were not quite sure what they were seeking. However, few students articulated a belief that they could go to librarians as they were trying to make decisions about what their topics might be, or how they might develop those topics via their research. A senior psychology major said, "I don't think I would see them and say, 'Well, this is my research, how can I do this and that?' I don't see them that way. I see them more like, 'Where's the bathroom?'" Our participant students did not always think of librarians as individuals with research expertise.

Seeking Help from Professors

Though students did not always know about or have relationships with librarians, students did know how teaching faculty can help them and actively sought professors' help. Students in our interviews saw their professors as experts in their disciplines and in the research process. Students also asked professors for help because they knew that professors exercised control over grades, and because students understood that part of the professors' role within the university was to help them. Having relationships structured in these ways—by students' perception of professors' expertise, by professors' power over students' grades, and by students' perception of professors' place within the university—professors were able to broker knowledge of the content of research and the research process. However, students may also have difficulties with some aspects of their research when assisted only by instructors.

In some cases, students seek professors for help because professors exercise power over them by determining their grades. A senior writing an environmental science paper said,

> I asked my professor for help because she's very—she has us using the LexisNexis database and she's very specific to her formatting and what she believes a research paper or outline or summary should look like, and by her being very specific to how she wants her paper written . . . like—an example with a paper that was worth 25 points, I got a 17—I wasn't happy with that because I always compare it to the class average. I saw the class had an average of 18, and I asked her, 'Okay, I chose the topic that you said you wanted us to research. Where did I lose points?" . . . She wanted more references [to] the ecosystem and [its] destruction . . . so had to rewrite my paper.

When professors define the rubrics, students reason, professors are the individuals to approach with questions. As a result, some students, like this one, are grade-oriented in their approach to their classes. Students may calculate the level of effort required to achieve the grades that they desire, including whether to approach a professor for help. Certainly not all students see their relationships with their professors in this way: a number of our students talked about going to their professors because they saw their professors' views as "good" or "correct," and this evaluation was not always present along with a grade orientation.

For whatever end students plan to use professors' help, students believe teaching faculty are knowledgeable about their research topics and about the research process. When asked where he would find books or articles for class, a civil engineering student said, "As books go, I'd probably talk to a professor or somebody who's knowledgeable on the topic, so if I need to do a history project on, like, France, I'd maybe talk to a French professor or something like that—ask them if they know of any books that would help me and then try and find them." When asked what kind of help a professor could provide, a criminal justice major said, "To see whether I'm headed off in the right direction, to see maybe if my—the quotes that I pull out support my argument well enough." A biology major said he asked for help with "how to strengthen . . . my thesis, or topic sentences, that sort of thing." Students' perception of professors' knowledge motivates students to seek professors for help.

Students also see professors as part of an established structure at the university to support their research. When asked why she did not typically ask librarians for assistance with research projects, one senior psychology major replied,

> I'm not used to. And . . . my feeling is they're not there to help me. I know it sounds kind of weird, but . . . I guess they're busy . . . they're busy doing something else, like . . . who am I to come and say? [With my] professor, I feel, at least I paid for the class and you're there to teach me this and I can at least use your office hours or something like that. With somebody that I have no connection [to] in any way it's like, why would I ask you?

This student understands that part of her professor's responsibilities is to help her. The teacher-student relationship is well-defined; librarians are believed to do work unrelated to helping students, or work that, while possibly related to research, does not entitle students to relationships with them.

Students' relationships with professors may have some surprising consequences for student help-seeking behavior, especially when combined with students' lack of knowledge of librarians' roles. For example, some students we interviewed assumed the topics in which they were interested were so specialized that they could only be discussed with professors. A junior taking a sociology class and writing about "men in white-collar jobs" explained why he went to his professor to ask for articles for his research project: "I think he was the only one that would know what I was writing about, because it was specific for that class . . . I think no other person would—could have helped me." Overestimating the specificity of their topics, and underestimating (or not even considering) librarians' ability to help, students will ask professors for help rather than librarians.

However, a student will not necessarily succeed in research if he or she relies on help from the professor alone. A number of professors with whom we spoke taught information literacy skills that librarians also teach, such as showing students how to use databases and how to narrow their topics through keyword searches. Some referred students to help from librarians, or incorporated library instruction into their classes. In these cases, students may have received the needed information literacy instruction. Other professors did not teach students how to use library resources or did not refer students to librarians for this instruction. These faculty members seemed to assume that students would pick up how to do library research, or that a one-shot instruction session, which at times professors erroneously assumed students previously had, would have been enough. At our universities, which students enter with wide ranges of preparedness for academic library use, the educational gap created by this relatively unsystematic approach may keep less-prepared students at a disadvantage.

Seeking Help from Peers and Family

Students were more eager to go to peers and to family for help than to seek librarians. To some extent, students' relationships with peers are determined by students' relationships with professors: students go to classmates in order to determine how to respond to their professors' expectations; in these ways, these helping relationships are influenced by students' relationships to the professor. However, students are also seeking help from peers and families because students are habitually in contact with them, and because students have been able to evaluate these individuals' likely knowledge of their research topics. Students' familiarity and positive experiences with peers and family mean that students will want to go to them for help. Nevertheless, peers and family may miseducate students about research.

In some cases, the type of relationship that students have with professors plays a role in how and whether students approach some of their peers. Here, classmates are seen as appropriate sources of help, as students assume that their classmates will also be attempting to puzzle through the assignments. A senior business major said,

> In the classroom, you know, everyone was pretty much checking with each other to make sure that someone didn't have like a way-out idea—just, say, "Okay, well, where are you at? Did you have any problems with the research information? . . . Were you finding incomplete materials? Original sources?"

Similarly, a junior biology major said, "I usually work with friends. So if I'm having trouble I ask them, 'How did you find this?' or, 'I'm not getting any data. Why are you?'" Students talk to each other about problems they are encountering, trying to ensure that they are progressing in approximately the same way, and helping each other with problems. This activity is not just about understanding the material, however. A freshman political science major said that he asked for help from a friend in order to "make sure it was up to the stats of the TA [teaching assistant]." When students compare their understanding and progress on assignments with each other they are helping each other, but they are also trying to meet their instructors' expectations. Students also go to peers and family for help because they are in relationships with these helpers, have received help from these individuals in the past, and find them accessible when help is needed. A freshman said she went to her friends for help because "they've helped me before with other stuff, yeah." A junior described "stressing out" with a friend about how they were going to find twenty sources as assigned for a project, at which point her friend helped her by walking her through the library website. In these cases, help seems to arise naturally in the context of ongoing interactions. A sophomore said she went to friends at school "because I'm always in a school environment." Although students described getting help from peers more frequently than they did from family, in both cases, students' help-seeking arose from established relationships.

The kind of familiarity that students have with peers and family allows students to make some critical evaluation of these individuals' ability to help. Students use such criteria as potential helpers' ages, education levels, or careers to justify their choices. A junior said, "I went to my dad and was like, 'Dad, help me,' because he has a bachelor's." A freshman said that he might ask his friends: "Usually I have friends who are older and in college and they definitely refer me to different sites or different sections in the library on how to find a book or maybe how to find a title." Familiarity provides students with access to knowledge about peers' and family members' potential to offer help.

However, when students get help from peers and family, they may be misinformed. Peers, for example, may influence each other to use the academic library, or they may lead each other to sources on the open Web instead. A senior sociology major said, "But my friends all use the Internet, and we don't go to the library. That's kind of why I think I feel comfortable not going. They don't do it. I don't really see why I should go too." A freshman said, "I had to ask someone who knows about—knows a lot about celebrities, which is a peer, a student in my same class . . . I asked her, 'Where is a good website to go to?' and she told me where to go. It's called Dogpile I believe . . . and so I went there and it helped me come up with more information for a paper." Students may, however inadvertently, connect each other to sources of information that are suboptimal or inappropriate.

Lacking University Supports for the Librarian-Student Relationship

Students may not seek help from librarians in part because our universities do not ensure that students and librarians connect with each other. Library instruction may not be required for students. As a result, relationships with professors, which are supported by the university, determine students' relationships with librarians. Faculty may have low expectations for librarians, and consequently students may not be connected to librarians or see why working with librarians may be helpful.

Our universities have introductory writing courses that can include library instruction led by librarians. Whether faculty use library instruction in these courses varies by university: at two universities, departments direct instructors to include library instruction in courses, and instruction sessions are written into the course curricula; at the other university, librarians encourage individual faculty members to include library instruction. There is also little to no penalty for instructors in these courses who choose not to offer library instruction. Outside the introductory writing courses, however, individual faculty members and departments determine whether classes include library instruction, or any introduction to information literacy. And, at our universities, which include transfer students who would not necessarily take these introductory courses, it is possible that some students do not receive library instruction at all. Ten percent, 12 percent, and 9 percent of students at DePaul, NEIU, and UIC, respectively, were incoming transfers in fall 2009 (DePaul Office of Planning and Institutional Research 2009; Northeastern Illinois University Office of Institutional Research 2009; University of Illinois at Chicago Office of Institutional Research 2009).

In the absence of an established structure ensuring that students build relationships with librarians throughout their college careers, professors play a critical role in brokering students' relationships with librarians. Some faculty members we interviewed chose to have instruction or to refer students to librarians, others did not, and some were unaware that some services, such as library instruction, were even offered by librarians. A number of our students who asked librarians for help said that they did so because their professors had told them about librarians or required them to go to librarians.

At the same time, professors can have low expectations for librarians' roles. When asked whom they thought students should ask for help, a number of faculty members said that they only expected students to ask faculty. One faculty member in religious studies explained,

> Well, I just really think it's my job . . . I've never had expectations of librarians. I know they have the reference desk but I just don't have the expectation because I just don't think the students use the librarians . . . Now I did get, once the librarian came into the class for an hour, I did get one or two really good students who made appointments with the librarian. But it's only going to be the good students, and they might have done it anyway.

When asked about librarians' roles in helping students, faculty also expressed low expectations of librarians' abilities as teachers and researchers. Some thought that librarians were only able to help students find information, believing that the librarian's primary job is, as one professor in communication studies said, "pointing out sources of information that are not the generic, standard ones that most people would think of." An anthropology faculty member said,

> I think that what happens is the librarians know how to search for sources, but sometimes don't know how to do research. And don't understand that by broadening the approach or taking a different angle or even sending the student back and saying, you know, "What are the other types of things [resources] you could look at to try to understand this problem?" Sometimes I don't know that the student's at a point where they can answer that question, but sometimes they are. And that's a common disjoint, I think. [Librarians] know how to try to search for things, but if it's not on topic they're gonna tell students, "Well there's nothing there. I don't know why you're even trying to find this stuff." And that's not what they [students] need to hear.

Faculty do not necessarily believe that librarians can help students learn the process of developing research interests by exploring related literatures.

If these low expectations for librarians are communicated to students, it may explain in part why some students ask their professors for help with all aspects of their projects, but have limited ideas about what they can request from librarians.

Seeking Help from Public Libraries

Students may not ask librarians for help because students' pursuit of help is shaped by their geography and history with certain libraries. (The undergraduate populations of the three Chicago universities in the ERIAL Project are composed largely of commuter students.) Our universities' students, many of whom attended Chicago public schools, ask for help at the same neighborhood public libraries that they used when writing papers in high school. When asked why she felt more comfortable asking librarians at the public library for help, a sophomore with an undeclared major said, "I guess because I've grown up by there, and I know . . . two librarians there." Students go to their public libraries because they are "convenient" to their homes, as a first-year student put it, and because they have established relationships with these librarians.

However, students using the public library may miss out on the depth of resources available at the academic library. A junior did not understand that the public library's collection may have been limited. She said, "I had to borrow books and one of the difficulties was I was going to the Chicago Public Library and you'd be surprised how many of them don't have research topic books. That was really difficult. . . ," she continued, explaining that "research topic books" were books related to the subject of her research paper. "So, I'd go and ask for help and they [the public library staff] would say, 'Oh we don't have that book. Maybe this branch does. You can try over there.'" Lacking an orientation to the college library and the help its librarians could provide, this student had difficulty finding the sources she needed.

Not Seeking Help

While some students' relationships lead them into help-seeking, some students' relationships, or lack of them, can lead them not to seek help at all. Some students in our study were having difficulties with which librarians could help them, but did not seek help from anyone. Of these, some students knew that they were having difficulty, but tried to be self-reliant, and others did not know they were in need of help.

Being Self-Reliant

In our sample, students who were having trouble sometimes tried to help themselves. A number of students talked about turning to Internet sources, including the library's online resources and the open Web. Students tended to prefer these sources because they were familiar and convenient, and possibly because those resources bolstered students' sense of independence. However, when students used the open Web they could run into difficulty finding the best sources, and they could have difficulty evaluating those sources.

When students are having trouble, they may turn to Internet sources for help, including the library's Web-based sources and the open Web. A junior public policy major said,

> I've noticed there aren't that many resources in the library or a lot of articles, so I've had to use the Internet, but from there I've actually found authors, reliable authors . . . PhDs doing research, so from there I can move on and figure out okay, with the few materials that are available at the library, how can I use them?

The open Web in particular is students' resource when they have difficulty using library resources, or when other sources fail them. A freshman who expressed reluctance to ask peers for help instead resorted to Google, saying, "I think just the Internet was my help."

Students prefer the Internet, especially the open Web, because it is familiar and convenient to them. In fact, students say that "of course" they go to the Internet, it is such an "obvious" source to them, referring to Google, for example, as "my trusty friend." A junior sociology major explained, "I've been using the Internet for, like, twelve years—I grew up with it, you know? So like, I'm at home there." A sophomore said, "I kind of always have gotten used to going on Google and just searching there."

The availability of open Web online resources such as Google and the library's Web resources may help students feel they can do their work independently. A sophomore English major said, "It's all on the library's website, so it's good that I went to the website and looked for it all. The instructions are really clear, but that's how I found it. Doing that on my own." A freshman appreciated the ease of access that JSTOR afforded him, saying, "You can use JSTOR wherever you go."

As with students accessing public libraries, self-reliant students, particularly those using the open Web, may miss out on the resources available in the academic library. Students using the open Web also have difficulty evaluating the credibility of Web-based resources, and find that website evaluation is a time-consuming process. A freshman elementary education major said of an Internet source:

> I'm not exactly sure who wrote it—I mean they do have things at the bottom where you can go and see the author, but they don't always have the most accurate information I find—especially when I was doing my research papers. It was good that I only had to use three Internet resources, because I had a tough time looking and just like I'm not exactly sure who are these people that are publishing it, and where they got the information from. It was kind of—in a book you always have other references, everything that they've used—in an Internet website I always find that it's kind of hard to follow those.

A junior said, "And, you know, you go on the Internet and you search for stuff and that's hard because you don't know what's actually been verified as true on the Internet because anybody can put anything on the Internet, so it's difficult." These students, though they feel more at home using the open Web, may at times be missing the most effective and efficient ways to find scholarly information.

Not Knowing When to Access Help

Some students in our study did not identify that they were having difficulties with which they could use help. Some overestimated their ability or knowledge. For example, a freshman electrical engineering student, when asked if there was anything else he would like to know about the library and its resources, said, without irony, "Not really, because I know it all." More commonly, students persevered as they tried to use library resources, but continued to have poor results without identifying if or when it would be appropriate to seek help. Students said, if they could have done something differently on their projects, that they probably would have spent more time on their work. Lacking orientation to the ways librarians could help them, these students devoted effort to ineffective research strategies.

DISCUSSION

These data suggest that analysis of undergraduate students' helping relationships inside and outside the library, and how these relationships are further shaped by universities, geography, and previous experience with information sources, can provide useful insights into their practices of help-seeking. We found that students did not ask librarians for help when they did not know how librarians could help them and when relationships with faculty and the structure of their universities offered only weak supports for ensuring that students build relationships with librarians. Instead, students prefer to seek help from those individuals with whom they have established relationships. Students may evaluate the knowledge of these individuals, but the relationships are also shaped by power and familiarity. Professors have power over students, and this power to some extent shapes the character of the relationship students have with the professor: since professors control students' grades, students see the professor as the logical choice from whom to seek help. Likewise, this relationship between student and professor shapes students' relationships with their peers somewhat, making classmates the other individuals deemed appropriate to ask questions. However, students also go to other peers and to family because students are familiar with these individuals, and students may go to public librarians for help because public librarians are both familiar and geographically convenient. In each of these relationships, students may be receiving the help that they need, but it is also possible that they do not receive appropriate help, either when a faculty member neglects to instruct a student in information literacy, when a peer miseducates a student, or when a public librarian is not able to offer all of the sources the student would need. We also find that some students do not seek help, either because they are self-reliant or because they do not perceive that they need help, and that a lack of help-seeking can also lead to difficulties in students' research.

Our findings reinforce prior research on help-seeking practices in libraries, specifically that students prefer to seek help from peers and professors rather than from librarians. In contrast to these earlier studies, which have identified categories of people from whom students seek help and students' experience and understanding of librarians and the library, our study also focused on the types of relationships associated with student help-seeking practices, as well as the influence of universities, geography, and other information sources. We believe our findings underscore the potential value of extending research on help-seeking to include a stronger focus on how relationships outside the library shape students' knowledge of and attitudes toward librarians in different universities, as well as the frequency and quality of interactions in relationships as factors in how students seek help.

WHAT ARE THE ANSWERS?

Given that some students do not seek substantive help from librarians, how can librarians become part of the academic support structure for college students? Given students' preference sometimes not to seek help at all, what can librarians do to support help-seeking as a learning strategy? Possible solutions to both these problems are to strengthen administrative structures ensuring the library is integrated into curricula, to capitalize on students' relationships with professors and peers, and to build relationships through online services.

As previously noted, administrative structures in these universities are not always in place to ensure that the library is part of students' college experience. Since students do not necessarily go to librarians as a source of help, libraries could focus their efforts on strengthening institutional structures at universities that support librarians' work. To do this, libraries could attempt, for example, to convince their university administrations that research classes with library instruction should be included as a necessary part of students' college experience. The challenge for building such a structure is a great one, and more research is needed to ensure that it is appropriate, such as longitudinal studies on the effectiveness of reference services and library instruction on students' research success.

This effort could also be furthered with quantitative analysis of how much contact students need to have with librarians in order to see them as appropriate sources of help with substantive reference questions, and whether giving the librarian further power over student assignments would substantially improve measures of student research success and the rate at which students access librarians. While our ethnographic data are suggestive, they are also limited in that, as in any ethnographic study, we do not know the extent to which our propositions hold true; we can only describe some real students' and professors' relationships and hypothesize how these data may be further generalized.

For librarians, building relationships with professors is critical for building relationships with students. Students go to professors for help. Librarians can build relationships with faculty to ensure that faculty recommend that students seek librarians for help. For example, in order to facilitate this process at NEIU, librarians recommended creating a checklist for marketing services to faculty, ensuring regular contacts to build these relationships, as well as hosting orientations for new faculty, who may be more open to learning about what library services are available to them. Since a number of students in our project went to the library when their faculty members required it, librarians can also approach faculty in order to create graded assignments that require work with librarians.

Peer mentors, that is, mentors to students who are students themselves, are also potential supporters and proponents of librarians. Some research supports this notion. Partnerships between peer mentors and librarians at Trinity University in Texas resulted in an increase in use of library sources and helped to establish student-librarian relationships (Millet and Chamberlain 2007). Sessions with peer mentors increased students' awareness of librarians and library sources. As a result of peer mentor training, several mentors brought their classes for library instruction. Peer mentors recognized when students needed help even when the professor did not. A recommendation from a classmate or friend may also determine whether students will use reference services in the future, even more than library instruction (Sobel 2009).

The NEIU Library is in the midst of working with the university's First Year Experience (FYE) program to train peer mentors to serve as conduits to the library and librarians. Peer mentors in the NEIU FYE program currently maintain a high level of interaction with first-year students. Mentors are committed to informing freshmen of services on campus and supporting them in the sometimes tumultuous transition from high school to college. Under the library's new initiative with the peer mentoring program, mentors will act as bridges between students and librarians, easing the anxiety related to approachability and access. The learning objectives of this project will first be met by the peer mentors themselves in order to ensure that they master the research skills that will be passed on to the students, and are as follows:

- Students will be able to locate materials and identify services in the library in order to increase their comfort level and familiarity with the library.
- Students will be able to identify, and articulate the advantages of using, library sources (online and print) in order to demonstrate their readiness for academic research.
- Students will be able to apply criteria to sources in order to evaluate the reliability, usefulness, or relevance of that source to their research.
- Students will see librarians as sources of help in order to expand their arsenal of academic support.

Peer mentors work only with first-year students, however, so librarians must seek other ways to ensure that all students are aware of the type of help that reference librarians can provide. As our research suggests, students' views of librarians' role in help-seeking may reflect the professors' view of the librarians' role. Students can be grade-oriented, so seeking assistance from a professor may appear to them to be a more logical approach than seeking help from someone outside of the student/professor/grade dynamic. Providing graded assignments that involve meeting with a reference librarian may incentivize students to seek help from librarians, making librarians part of a circle of support that students view not only as accessible, but as logical.

Students also view the Internet as an accessible source of help although they may at times question the trustworthiness of the content. The plethora of information sources available online and their relative ease of access give students a sense of autonomy and self-control that feels liberating and empowering. Librarians can work with this sense of self-efficacy by weaving our presence into their Web world via chat reference, online guides and tutorials, and other tools that will connect them to the library from where they are already connected.

CONCLUSIONS

Students will seek help from those with whom they have established relationships. Those relationships have either developed over time, as with friends and family, or are etched into existing power structures such as that between the professor and the student. Relationships with librarians can start early in students' college years and build over time. The long-term outcomes of such relationships need to be further studied and documented; however, fostering such relationships may be beneficial. For example, when asked why they were comfortable asking a librarian for help, one freshman replied,

> Pretty much because when we did a tour when I was doing the summer transition program [a program to introduce students to the college campus], when we came to the library . . . because she [the librarian introducing students to the library] was so nice, and she explained how you know, all the librarians here are very nice, and when somebody's at the reference desk they want to help us . . . and all of them, all the people are so nice and just made you feel really, really comfortable just to ask even a simple question, and just made everybody feel so comfortable . . .

This student felt comfortable asking a librarian for help because she had been introduced to the library and the librarians during a summer program for incoming freshmen. Positive interactions such as these are a step toward creating student-librarian relationships based on familiarity, a factor that our study suggests influences students' willingness to seek assistance. With institutional support, librarians can foster these kinds of relationships via peer mentor programs, graded library assignments that emerge from librarian-faculty collaborations, and increased librarian outreach efforts to meet students in-person and online. In this way, librarians position themselves to work with other departments, programs, and campus initiatives so that seeking help from librarians is not only encouraged, but essential.

NOTE

1. Students' tendency not to ask librarians for help may be a growing trend. The Association for Research Libraries Statistics 2007–2008 suggests that reference transactions in its member libraries decreased by 53 percent between 1991 and 2007 (Kyrillidou and Bland 2009), though there is debate about how accurately such data reflect how librarians currently provide reference services (for example, see Novotny 2002).

5

Searching for Answers: Student Research Behavior at Illinois Wesleyan University

ANDREW D. ASHER AND LYNDA M. DUKE

Locating and evaluating information is an essential skill for academic success. Moreover, the ability to conduct a successful and efficient search for high-quality information is a critical thinking skill that is central to life in contemporary information and knowledge-driven environments. Search has, of course, become part of our daily lives like never before, as Internet search engines play an ever-increasing role in how we locate and process information. However, the seeming simplicity of tools like Google belies a complex and iterative process that requires the integration of numerous analytical and technical steps, as well as knowledge and experience on the part of the user.

When searching for scholarly resources for an academic assignment, successful students must not only familiarize themselves with a discipline and its particular jargon, but also must have an adequate understanding of how information is organized, how to evaluate sources, and how to use the "tools" of scholarship, such as online catalogs, databases, indexes, Library of Congress Subject Headings, and many of the other myriad resources available in an academic library. If a student lacks sufficient knowledge in any one of these areas, the quality of their search results, and subsequently the sources on which they base their research, can be significantly diminished.

Recent studies have suggested several trends in the search habits of undergraduate students. According to an OCLC summary of user behavior reports, Google and electronic journals are playing an ever-increasing role in the research process (Connaway and Dickey 2010, 4). Google's place as the preferred starting point for both everyday and academic research is clear, as evidenced by almost every recent study of student search habits (Connaway and Dickey 2010, 28–29; Head and Eisenberg 2009, 15; De Rosa et al. 2005, 1–7; Prabha, Connaway, and Dickey 2006, 13–14, 16–18; Griffiths and Brophy 2005, 550, 545). This is not to say, however, that students are using Google for everything. Even if students begin with Google, there is evidence from both the ERIAL study and elsewhere (Gabridge, Gaskell, and Stout 2008, 516–17; Head and Eisenberg 2009, 3) that students working on academic assignments do eventually consult library databases, especially when seeking reliable or scholarly sources.

Google's pervasiveness may also be affecting search in other more subtle ways. Google's simplicity and single search box seems to have created the expectation among students of a specific search experience within the library: in particular, a single search box that quickly accesses many resources and an overreliance on simple keyword search (see Hampton-Reeves et. al. 2009, 45; CIBER 2008, 14).

In comparison with the ease of the Google user experience, the various and fragmented catalogs, databases, and interfaces contained on a typical academic library's website are extremely complex. The "cognitive load" of using these resources effectively can be "immense" (CIBER 2008, 30), thereby inhibiting students' successful retrieval of information (see Wong et. al. 2009, 6). As nonexpert and nonprofessional researchers, undergraduate students typically emphasize efficiency over thoroughness (Head and Eisenberg 2009, 20; Griffiths and Brophy 2005, 549–50; Connaway and Dickey 2010, 32, 34), and favor full-text online resources (see also Connaway and Dickey 2010, 27). This can be viewed as searching using the path of least resistance, in which luck plays an important role and a willingness to settle for "good enough" sources is student researchers' accepted practice.

This chapter will examine how undergraduates at Illinois Wesleyan University find and evaluate information for their research assignments.[1] As part of the ERIAL Project, the IWU research team conducted two types of interviews that specifically investigated how students search: research process interviews and ethnographic interviews (for a description of these methods, see chapter 1). In total, 60 IWU undergraduate students participated in these interviews: 30 in each of the two types. First-year students accounted for just under half this sample with 29 participants, while sophomores, juniors, and seniors were more evenly represented with 12, 7, and 10 participants respectively (2 students did not indicate their academic level).

Although the ERIAL research team observed a considerable range in students' search capabilities, and a few students demonstrated excellent search skills, the majority of students—of all levels—who participated in this study exhibited significant difficulties that ranged across nearly every aspect of the search process. In general, students appeared to lack the methodological understanding required to conduct an effective search. After reviewing IWU's research process interviews, only 7 out of 30 students conducted what a librarian might consider a reasonably well-executed search. Search therefore appears to be a significant area of weakness for IWU students, and many students described experiences of anxiety and confusion when looking for resources—an observation that seems to be widespread among students at the five institutions involved in the study. When asked to describe the biggest problems she encountered when working on research assignments, a senior in music replied,

Probably finding a topic. 'Cause I'm always afraid that [it] doesn't have enough literature . . . that I won't find enough sources for [it], or that it's going to be too complex for me and I will find sources, but I won't be able to understand them and then I won't be able to write a thesis because I don't know what they are talking about. So that's always my fear: like I'll pick a topic and I'll be working on it and several weeks go by and that's when I realize it's too hard and I won't have as much time to write the paper and change the topic.

Similarly, a senior in women's studies described her confusion in conducting a search:

> Just finding ways to narrow down, there was just so much information
> . . . how do I weed out what my specific topic is from the general larger
> topic? . . . How do I find specifically my information when there's not
> a book titled [on] this topic? So, I guess just being overwhelmed with
> the amount of literature out there [that] doesn't really relate to my
> topic and how do I pull my stuff out of it? 'Cause I feel like I was very
> much kind of blindly branching out and a lot of times by chance finding
> things and then going on from there.

Unfortunately, these difficulties appear to flow directly from gaps in students' information literacy skills. In the following pages we will discuss some of the most significant deficiencies we observed in students' search strategies, as well as suggestions for addressing these issues.

CHOOSING A DATABASE

Students routinely exhibited difficulties finding and choosing an appropriate database for their research. Of the 30 research process interviews, 15 students conducted searches in databases that a librarian would most likely never recommend for their topic. Furthermore, students who had not had a library instruction session exhibited substantial difficulty finding their way to any library database. For example, while looking for a journal article, one student tried the following areas on the library's website: ILLiad (used to request journal articles not owned by IWU), Digital Commons (the institutional repository), Citation Linker (used to locate journal titles owned by the library), the I-Share catalog (used to request books from other Illinois libraries), and Google, where she finally gave up without locating an article.

When choosing a database, students typically returned repeatedly to a resource that had worked in the past, even if it was not the best or most appropriate for the task (see also Head and Eisenberg 2009, 3). The Ames Library's usage statistics also reflected this. Of the 101 databases that had one year of comparable search data, the top three databases (JSTOR, PsycINFO, and Academic Search Premier) accounted for 38.7 percent of searches. Usage then fell off quickly, with the next seven databases accounting for 20.4 percent of searches. The remaining 91 databases accounted for 40.9 percent of searches, with 76 of these databases holding a less than 1 percent share of total searches (table 5.1).[2]

The popularity of JSTOR is perhaps illustrative. At IWU, JSTOR appears to have a very loyal following. During our ethnographic interviews, JSTOR was mentioned 56 times, followed distantly by PsycINFO with 17 mentions. Only Google exceeded JSTOR, with 115 references. Students appeared to rely on JSTOR disproportionately, to an extent that surprised the librarians, who often did not view JSTOR as the optimum resource for students' research assignments. However, for students, JSTOR was usually sufficiently robust to meet the minimum requirements of a particular assignment—typically around five sources. In short, JSTOR simply works for a wide range of assignments across a wide range of disciplines, providing fast access to full-text and reliable resources. Students generally

TABLE 5.1 *Database Use at IWU, Academic Year 2008–2009*

Database	Number of Searches	Percentage of Total Searches
JSTOR	32,116	14.78%
PsycINFO	27,906	12.84%
Academic Search Premier	24,082	11.08%
Top 3	84,104	38.7%
CINAHL Plus with full text	9481	4.36%
Hoover's Online	6501	2.99%
MLA International Bibliography	6190	2.85%
Science Citation Index	5789	2.66%
LexisNexis	5515	2.54%
Social Sciences Citation Index	5478	2.52%
Arts & Humanities Citation Index	5400	2.49%
Top Ten	128,458	59.11%
Remaining 91 Databases	88,840	40.88%
TOTAL	434,596	100%

did not realize—and had not investigated—the limitations of the database that might make it inappropriate for a given task. For example, students regularly used JSTOR to search for current information, not realizing that JSTOR does not provide access to the most recently published articles (articles typically only appear in JSTOR after 3–5 years, depending on publisher).[3] Nor did students think to investigate whether or not there was a database that would be more focused on their topic of choice. Students found JSTOR effective because it fit in well with their established work practices. Unfortunately, because it provides access to full-text materials, as well as its flexibility and wide coverage of topics, JSTOR also enabled students to succeed using subpar search strategies simply because it worked well enough.

Making search easier for students can therefore be a double-edged sword: while it enables students to get to information faster and easier, it can also reinforce unreflective research habits that contribute little to the overall synthesis of a research paper or academic argument.

CONSTRUCTING A SEARCH

Once students chose a database (that was appropriate or otherwise) for their search activities, they often did not understand how to use it adequately. Almost without exception, IWU students exhibited a lack of understanding of search logic, how to build a search to narrow or expand results, how to use subject headings, and how various search engines (including Google) organize and display results. As one student mentioned while conducting a search of the library's online catalog, "Apparently you don't have much on rock and roll," not realizing that if she changed her search term (i.e., to rock music), she would have encountered many excellent sources for her assignment.

During the 30 research process interviews conducted for the ERIAL study, the research team observed 121 unique searches.[4] Ninety-three of these searches were for unknown items (e.g., when a student was attempting to discover sources related to a research question, rather than a specific book title or journal article).

The vast majority of searches we observed students conduct were simple searches. Students generally treated all search boxes as the equivalent of a Google search box, and searched "Google-style," using the "any word anywhere" keyword search as a default. Of the 30 students we observed, 27 conducted searches using "any word anywhere," "all fields," or an equivalent default search when it was not appropriate to do so. In total, 155 of the 192 observed sets of search terms used this approach (see also CIBER 2008, 14; Hampton-Reeves et. al. 2009, 45). While searching in the CINAHL database, a junior in nursing explained, "So, I basically throw whatever I want into the search box and hope it comes up . . . But it's like Google and I use it like Google. I don't know how to use it any other way."

Students' overuse of the simple search leads directly to the problems of obtaining too many or too few search results. These twin problems of "too little" and "too much" information are really one and the same, as both issues stem from a lack of sufficient conceptual understanding of how information is organized and how to build an effective search query in library databases. Almost all of the students we interviewed exhibited difficulties evaluating and narrowing down (or expanding) search results.

When faced with unsatisfactory results, students usually changed the search, either by entering new search terms or trying a different database altogether, rather than using more advanced search tools to expand or refine the search. Perhaps because of their experience with Google, students often appeared to believe that if they could only find the magic words or phrase, whatever piece of information they were looking for would be revealed to them.

This belief can cause students to assume that if they cannot quickly find information on a topic, then the information must not exist and they should give up on that topic. Only rarely did students conclude that a lack of search results might, in fact, reflect incorrect search terms or an ineffective search strategy. A sophomore international studies major noted,

> Originally I had a different topic. I was thinking about something that had to do [with] the discrimination of Jews in sixteenth-century London, and I realized that *finding information on that would be almost impossible.* 'Cause I'm interested in the really obscure topics that you would be like, "that's really interesting." But no one really has done anything on that, so it's really hard to find. So, [crime in nineteenth-century London] seemed like it would be easy to find information on, so I decided on that one and I was interested [in it] [italics added].

Students regularly overestimated how "obscure" a particular topic actually is, and demonstrated remarkable ease in changing topics to fit easily found information. In this way, students pass up unique or interesting topics in favor of topics with widespread coverage.

When asked how many sources she would look at before changing her research topic, the international studies student above replied, "Probably, it would depend on time. I probably would take about an hour and say if I can't find any websites, articles, anything in an hour's time, then it's just pointless, you shouldn't do it. Usually doing Google, if you change your keywords 3, 4, or 5 times and still nothing pops up, then you know you should change your topic. There's really nothing going on there." She continued, noting her tendency to change topics as a result of a failed search:

> Well lots of times, when you're looking for websites or articles, you'll find one that's really credible and good, so you automatically think you don't have to keep looking anymore, I found it, it's good. And then you start looking through it and find out it's some 17 year old that just made this website and all this. So sometimes you get discouraged and you think that maybe you should just pick another topic. I know a couple of times I was like, "I don't think this is going to work out, I should start talking to my professor about another topic." So, it really takes a lot of reading the books and really going through them and going through the articles and making sure you can use them.

Throughout the ERIAL Project's interviews, we observed students fitting their research papers to sources, rather than using sources as a basis for furthering an argument. Students assumed that any information obtained from the library website is automatically "good," and often allowed the first few sources they located to define their research question. In general, students had a very strong preference for selecting sources that were available online in full-text, often leading to a student ignoring a potentially appropriate source simply because it was not readily available. Indeed, any barrier, even the most mundane or rudimentary, could inhibit students from accessing a particular source (see also CIBER 2008, 30). For example, requesting an item through interlibrary loan, finding a print source in the stacks, or even clicking on a link to another database were routinely viewed as obstacles not worth the effort of navigating. A senior in women's studies commented: "When I get somewhere where it says, 'Oh, this isn't available here, do this to request it,' I'm just like, 'let's see if I can find this somewhere else without [requesting it].' I pretty much pick the least amount of work necessary. If I don't have access to it, I search for something else."

IWU students were equally plagued by too much information, and found themselves overwhelmed by a deluge of search results that they were often unequipped to evaluate, limit, and refine. A first-year student in music studies related how he often feels overwhelmed by information. When asked what he expected librarians to know about technology, he explained,

> How to use it and how not to let it distract you. How to keep [information] under control. [I need to] not sit there on an information binge for an hour—Be able to say "okay, I've used [the databases]; I actually need to read these sources now." I actually didn't feel like I got that feeling in our [library] information sessions, [when] it was a little bit more like [the way] we need to be researching. And, literally, I would come in here and literally for hours be researching. I finally realized, "whoa, I need to just read some of these things." Because I had this much paper printed out (spreads fingers to about 1") and like 15 books, seriously. And I needed to slow down on the research.

A junior in psychology also explained his difficulty conducting the literature review for one of his papers:

> So for me [the literature review] was kind of hard, the one big thing that a lot of people actually commented on was "how are we supposed to know what's out there?" It's really hard to just search, because you can be searching and searching and then oftentimes you can try different keywords and it will bring this wealth of information that you could easily be overlooking if you didn't do an exhaustive search, which is what we always heard [that we should do]. But how are you supposed to know what's out there? . . . Because sometimes you wouldn't find anything on what you were supposed to talk about or you couldn't find anything on what you wanted to talk about. So the information is there and the system is there but I think, as students, it's hard to pull it out because there's so much out there."

These struggles indicate that students need tools that help provide structure to their searches. In our observations, students tended to have greater success when they were forced to choose subject keywords through a guided keyword process (e.g., PsycINFO) or when facets were available to easily refine results.

SOURCE EVALUATION: "I NEVER GO PAST THE FIRST PAGE"

Students' evaluation of potential sources appeared cursory (see also CIBER 2008, 10). Students typically made rapid appraisals of a source's usefulness, often based only on its title or a superficial scan of its abstract. Only rarely did a student actually look at the subject headings or keywords associated with the document, read the text itself, or locate the book to review the table of contents. For example, one student, while searching library databases for information about women in baseball, lamented the dearth of information about this subject and was seriously considering changing topics—all while her mouse was hovering over the subject heading "All-American Girls Professional Baseball League."

When evaluating search results, students seldom examined citations past the first or second page of their results, an observation that is supported by Griffiths and Brophy's recent study of search engine use (2005, 551). A senior in psychology explained while demonstrating a search,

> Honestly I never go past 2 or 3 pages in searching for the results. But if I find something that I like, I look at the title and if the title seems applicable, I look at the abstract and if that looks applicable, I go through and read a little bit more of the introduction and if that seems applicable then I'll print it. I don't like these ones that came up, so I'm going to search something else.

When evaluating sources, students also utilized eclectic, and sometimes inaccurate, methods of source evaluation, particularly when examining the validity of websites (see also Lee 2008, 215). A first-year student in mathematics described how she decided on the credibility of a website:

If I can make it, I wouldn't trust it. [Pointing to a website on parenting as an example] I can probably make this website; I probably wouldn't be able to make this part [pointing], but I mean everything else. Like this neon blue background with that font and just put stuff [on the page]. I wouldn't use this website, I would use the book where it's published or some other scholarly articles or if it's Princeton Study or something like that, anything to do with the word scholarly, school, or university I would probably use.

A sophomore in music education observed,

I don't know. I am probably not the best person for this, but I just look at the bottom and see if there's an address or some kind of seal and—simple—if it says association or foundation or something, I assume that someone is saying that it's worth it. I don't know. Overall on a website, it's pretty easy to see if you paid to have a web designer to do this website, or if you just kind of made it on iWeb. So that's probably not the best way, but. . .

When searching for sources for an academic paper, students routinely searched only to meet the minimum expectations of the assignment rather than the most relevant or most useful sources. Students tended to make use of whatever materials were most easily available, and focused more on simply finishing a paper and getting a grade, than questions of research process. When asked what resources she used to write a paper, the mathematics student replied, "Websites mostly. Ideally I would use books 'cause books you can take home with you. It's nice but it's not as easy as a website, but you know books are reliable. It's been through so many people and everything so if I was looking for reliability, books would be better. But I'm lazy and I use the Internet."

Furthermore, IWU students often did not try, or allow enough time, to have a comprehensive approach to literature review. The mathematics first-year student continued, "I usually have one or two main sources [that] I get a lot of my information from and then others where I get the rest of them like [to fill] the cracks that I need . . . Yeah I procrastinate, but when I want something, I want it now."

A senior in accounting also admitted that she did not want to commit the time required to do thorough research,

I don't want to be reading a lot of old stuff . . . like an article—it's bad enough to read through like 15 pages, I don't want to have to flip through an entire book. And especially if it's gonna be like these 10 books that I get and each book has 3 pages in it, so I get to carry around 10 books just so I can read these 30 pages. So I don't know. I guess that's probably laziness more than anything else.

TECHNICAL PROBLEMS

While IWU students exhibited the most significant problems with information literacy and the intellectual aspects of search, students also encountered a variety of technical difficulties when navigating the various and fragmented databases and interfaces of the library, including dead links in the databases, slow database interfaces, and incomplete information on ILLiad (document) request forms. These problems often resulted in students abandoning the source in question and beginning a search for different items. As observed above, students were very quick to give up on pursuing a source, so much so, that virtually any obstacle they encountered would cause them to move on to another source or to change their research topic.

Students also exhibited a lack of understanding of where the border is located between library resources and Internet resources. For example, when a student is instructed by a professor to find "non-Internet sources," students are often unsure if the library databases, which are accessed via the Internet, constitute appropriate sources. Likewise, if a student accesses library resources via Google Scholar, the student is often unaware that these are, in fact, frequently made available through the library (see also CIBER 2008, 16).

Students who had participated in library instruction sessions clearly knew more about the search process than those who had not. These students were more adept at locating databases, changing keywords, and using more of the library's tools. As one student noted, the librarian "gives us the most effective sources to use." Likewise, a senior in psychology explained the importance of library information sessions:

I was introduced to how to find scholarly articles and journals. And I literally had no idea before. I would have been Googling for the past four years if they hadn't told me. That's pretty huge, I think. They taught us how to expand or explode—I don't know the term, but your search terms. So you can look for more and narrow it and how to limit your searches to exactly what you want. Just kind of [the] functionality of the program.

Nevertheless, even students who had participated in information sessions often did not remember some basic or specific concepts, or apply them correctly.

SEEKING HELP

Although the majority of IWU students struggled with finding the correct database to use, their search terms, locating a known item, and/or technical problems, not one student sought the assistance of a librarian during an observed search. This result corresponds with the findings of Project Information Literacy, a national study of college students' information-seeking behaviors, which reported that "eight out of 10 of the respondents reported rarely, if ever, turning to librarians for help with course-related assignments," while only "1 in 10 students used online reference, or non-credit library sessions" (Head and Eisenberg 2009, 3, 23). Though vexing, this may not, however, be a new problem. Fister, in her 1992 study of the undergraduate research process, observed that students sought out instructors, rather than librarians, for help during different stages of the research process (Fister 1992, 4, 6, 10); an observation that was confirmed throughout the ERIAL study (see chapter 4).

However, the IWU students we observed did ask for help at the library's three service points (all of which are staffed by student assistants) for technical assistance, such as when they encountered difficulty finding a book in the stacks or a jammed printer. Students generally exhibited significant difficulty locating books in the library stacks, often resulting in a failed search. Unfortunately, when students sought help for locating a book at the library's service points, they were sometimes given incomplete or incorrect information, indicating a need for more intensive training of the student service workers.

CONCLUSIONS

The ERIAL Project provided the first opportunity for librarians at IWU to systematically understand how their students conduct their research, using both library databases as well as search engines on the Internet. While we anticipated that students would rely on Google and the Internet for much of their searching, and that they would find library systems more time-intensive and difficult to use, we were surprised at the extent to which students appeared to lack even some of the most basic information literacy skills that we assumed they would have mastered in high school: understanding how information is organized, evaluating sources appropriately, and how best to access library-owned sources (books included). Moreover, and perhaps most frustrating for librarians, students showed an almost complete lack of interest in seeking assistance from librarians during the search process.

Upon reflection, this overall lack of understanding on the part of IWU students could possibly be viewed as a reasonable response to their successful experiences in utilizing the Internet to fulfill their information-seeking needs, with little need to understand or investigate how search engines actually work. Additionally, because searching Google is so easy and almost always yields results, the need to seek out assistance has been greatly reduced. This could also help to explain the lack of interest (or perceived need) to seek out help from librarians.

A number of ideas have been identified at IWU to help address the areas of concern that were documented as a result of the ERIAL Project. Even before the official end of the study (in summer 2010), the Ames Library faculty and staff began the process of implementing a number of initiatives, including completely revamping the information literacy program, rethinking how to more effectively market library resources and services, placing a renewed emphasis on training student assistants, a careful review of databases and other tools of scholarship for ways to de-fragment these services, and fine-tuning of the library's web pages. Chapter 9 gives a more complete description of the process for identifying, prioritizing, and implementing these issues.

Ethnographic techniques proved especially useful for holistically understanding students' research processes and practices at IWU, as well as providing a fine-grained tool for analyzing the obstacles students encountered when conducting research. These interviews vividly demonstrated what students are actually doing on real assignments in real time, as well as how students choose to handle various impediments along the way.

Because of the invaluable data collected during this project, the library faculty at IWU is committed to establishing a continuous data-collection strategy that will build a significant longitudinal data set to use in evaluating our instructional and service interventions. As such, librarians are currently developing a standardized interview protocol to further ensure that these research results remain comparable over time. Because of the complex processes involved in searching for information, as well as the diverse array of problems this study observed in students' research practices, the problem of how to best incorporate the teaching of information literacy concepts and skills within student instruction will continue to be a central issue for IWU. Our goal is to build on the substantial data gathered during the ERIAL Project to create a sustainable research program to further develop our understanding of the research needs of our students, as well as to gauge our success in meeting these needs.

NOTES

1. Illinois Wesleyan University is a highly selective, private, liberal arts school with 2,100 undergraduate students.

2. These statistics encompass usage by the entire university. Unfortunately, it is impossible to differentiate student searches from other users. However, given that IWU students vastly outnumber faculty, it is reasonably safe to assume that this usage is student-driven.

3. This will change in 2011 when JSTOR will begin offering a "Current Scholarship Program" containing up-to-date content from 174 journal titles.

4. For the purposes of our analysis, we defined a search as any time a student opened a new resource to search for information. If the student changed his search terms within a resource, we did not count this as a new search. Therefore we observed 121 searches encompassing 192 separate sets of search terms.

6

Supporting the Academic Success of Hispanic Students

DAVID GREEN

Serving Latino students is about intentionality. It means knowing the profile of the Latino population at your institution and in your community. It means knowing the performance of your Latino students and identifying their strengths and needs. It means considering adaptations to curricular design, academic, and support services to increase retention or promote persistence for your Latino students. Serving Latino students means graduating your Latino students. Serving Latino students does not mean institutions serve them at the expense of other students. This is not an either/or proposition. Rather, institutions can build on what works in serving Latino students to better serve other students as well. (Santiago 2009, 20)

Even if your institution only enrolls a small number of Hispanic students, I want to suggest several reasons that this chapter is still relevant to you and the work that you do at your library. First, the number of Hispanic students is growing at a significant rate in the United States, and their enrollment numbers will increase at institutions of higher education throughout North America (Gandara and Contreras 2009, 2). Second, the success of Hispanic students in higher education has been identified as an issue of national importance in the United States for the overall health of the country (Gandara and Contreras 2009, 2). Finally, the changes in the library we are pursuing at Northeastern Illinois University to enhance the success and engagement of Hispanic students are relevant to the success of all students, not just Hispanic students.

What is stressed repeatedly in the literature on Hispanic students is that to effectively serve this student population, educators must make the effort to learn about them. That is to say, not to learn just about Hispanic students in general, but about *your* Hispanic students specifically. This chapter will discuss the various qualitative and quantitative methods we used at NEIU to understand the needs of our Latino students and how we intend to use that information to make our library services more effective.

WHO IS "HISPANIC"?

Who are we talking about when we use the term *Hispanic*? This term has different meanings to different people and is a complex issue. The U.S. Census Bureau relies entirely on self-reporting and leaves the definition of *Hispanic* up to the individual. For the Census Bureau, you are Hispanic if you say you are Hispanic, and if you say you are not Hispanic, then you are not.

> In the eyes of the Census Bureau, Hispanics can be of any race, any ancestry, any country of origin. The result is that there are varying patterns relating to where people come from and how they choose to identify themselves on the Census. For example, some 99% of all immigrants from Mexico call themselves Hispanic. But just 87% of immigrants from Venezuela adopt this label, as do 86% of immigrants from Argentina, 70% of immigrants from Spain, and only 67% from Panama. As for race, 54% of all Hispanics in the U.S. self-identify as white, 1.5% self-identify as black, 40% do not identify with any race and 3.8% identify as being two or more races. (Passel and Taylor 2009, 3)

On the other hand, based on a law passed in 1976 by the U.S. Congress to collect and analyze data on "Americans of Spanish origin or descent," the Office of Management and Budget developed a very specific definition for "Hispanics or Latinos." This definition is also used for the Integrated Postsecondary Education Data System.

> The language of that legislation described this group as "Americans who identify themselves as being of Spanish-speaking background and trace their origin or descent from Mexico, Puerto Rico, Cuba, Central and South America and other Spanish-speaking countries." This is the definition used by "schools, health facilities and other government entities and agencies [to] keep track of how many Hispanics they serve." (Passel and Taylor 2009, 2)

The terms *Hispanic* and *Latino* (used interchangeably in this chapter) may not be easy to concisely define. What is far more important is to recognize the tremendous diversity of peoples such an umbrella can include.

> [Hispanic] students differ markedly in terms of culture and geographic origin in different parts of the country. In California and Texas, they are most likely Chicano or Mexican. In Florida and New York they are most likely Cuban or Puerto Rican. And in an increasing number of regions, they may be immigrants from Central or South America. "Hispanic" students may also differ substantially based on how long they or their families have lived in the United States. For example, the families of some students in Texas, New Mexico, and the San Luis Valley in Colorado have resided in those areas for hundreds of years. The families of other students may have been here for one or two generations, while still others have only recently immigrated. Some students are bilingual and some claim English as their first language; some are economically disadvantaged while others are middle-class. These cross-cutting differences are important for college leaders to understand when contemplating the many ways to improve student success. (American Association of State Colleges and Universities 2007, 10)

In this case, the "local population" we want to consider includes graduate and undergraduate Hispanic students who are enrolled at NEIU.

THE PROCESS OF LEARNING ABOUT LATINO STUDENTS

Initially, the NEIU team separated and analyzed all the data from the self-identified Hispanic students who had participated in the ERIAL Project at NEIU. The data at this level of observation and inquiry showed that these students were almost identical to their peers at NEIU. Upon reflection, we realized we still needed additional information to better understand these students, much of it quantitative.

The research team contacted NEIU's Office of Institutional Research (OIR) to learn more about the Latino student population. We discovered that the general academic profile for Latino students (high school GPA, ACT scores, and so forth) was almost identical to the averages for the student body at large. The only striking difference was that male Latinos had a significantly lower six-year degree program completion rate. For the fall 2003 first-time, full-time freshman cohort class, the six-year degree program completion rate for male Latino students was 13.0 percent, 19.2 percent for Latinas, and 20.4 percent for the cohort as a whole (the 2003 freshman cohort consisted of 1,046 students, 396 of whom were Hispanic).

In addition, the general demographic information collected by this office did not indicate many differences from the overall student population at NEIU. Significant to note, however, is that of the Latino students, 63 percent are female, and 90 percent graduated from high schools in the greater Chicago area. At least 50 percent of our Hispanic students are transfer students from other Chicago-area universities and colleges. Looking at the most popular declared majors of the undergraduate Hispanic students provides a sense of where their interests lay: 16 percent of the male Hispanic students who have declared a major chose justice studies; 20 percent of the female Hispanic students chose teacher education. All other majors had significantly lower rates of selection.

Although NEIU's OIR was able to provide us with some academic and demographic data, it was unable to cover all of our areas of interest. Because 90 percent of our Latino students are from the Chicago area, we then reviewed the U.S. Census data for more detailed information.

There are several research institutes which provide a variety of reports and analyses on the Latino population in the Chicago area which proved helpful. Table 6.1 lists the origins of Latino populations which account for 1 percent or more of the Latino population in the Chicago Metro area, as described in one of the reports produced by the Institute of Latino Studies at the University of Notre Dame (Alejo 2008, 7).

Almost 80 percent of the Latino population in Chicago has origins from Mexico. Thus, it is likely that the majority of our Latino students have families which emigrated from Mexico. In addition, according to the census data from 2006, 89 percent of the Latino population in Chicago under the age of 18 was born in the United States and 63 percent of those 18 or older were foreign born. This would indicate that most of our students are probably either first or second generation (see http://pewhispanic.org/files/factsheets/13.pdf for a discussion on this topic).

Furthermore, only 24 percent of U.S.-born Latinos and 9 percent of the foreign-born Latinos had a college education. More important, 55 percent of the foreign-born Latinos had not completed high school. It is also important to note that 27 percent of the Latino population in Chicago speaks little or no English. Determining how many of our own Hispanic students have parents who speak little English is also an important component in understanding our students' needs.

We are in the process of working with our OIR and various teaching faculty to create a survey instrument designed to help us learn more about the NEIU Latino population. When we collect demographic information

TABLE 6.1 *Metro Chicago Latino Population by Specific Origin, 2006*

Origin	Number	Percentage of Latino Population
Hispanic or Latino	1,722,843	100.00%
Mexican	1,357.353	78.79%
Puerto Rican	153,206	8.89%
Guatemalan	30,332	1.76%
Cuban	18,875	1.10%
Ecuadorian	18,796	1.09%
Colombian	16,482	0.96%

from our Hispanic students next year, we anticipate that we will find that most of our students are second-generation immigrants or generation 1.5,[1] and a significant percentage of them have parents that never completed high school. Our goal is to gather this information in a campus-wide survey of all our students in the spring of 2011.[2] This information will be instrumental in helping not just the library, but all departments on campus design and deliver better services to this population.

MEET MARIA

Using information gathered from three sources—our ethnographic instruments, data from OIR, and data from the Census Bureau—I would like to present a composite profile of an NEIU Latino student and her experience using the NEIU library during a typical weekend.

Maria is a sophomore at NEIU studying social work. She works about twenty hours a week helping out in her aunt's shop, although during busy seasons she has to put in many more hours. She had to take a year off from college after her freshman year to help at home when her mother became severely ill. Once her mother recovered she returned to the university to pursue her degree.

When Maria returned to her studies, she enrolled in two courses at the El Centro campus, which is about 4 miles from the main campus of NEIU. There are no library services, collections, or staff at the El Centro campus. Maria's high school didn't have a librarian, but there was a library room with some books in it and a few computers. She never needed to use the school library because she found all the information she needed for her high school papers at the public library near where she lived. She had been visiting that library since she was a little girl and was familiar with most of the staff members' faces. She knew who to go to for help when she needed it.

One of the classes that Maria had this semester was an anthropology class which required her to write a research paper. The instructor had put some materials on reserve at the library on the main campus, which was required reading for the class. She decided to go to the library to access the required readings and do a little research for her paper.

On Saturday, Maria took public transportation from her home to go to the library on the main campus. It took her a little over an hour and a half to get there. Unfortunately, it rained on the way so she arrived on campus with soggy shoes and a bit chilled. She thought she might try to get a cup of hot coffee or cocoa to warm her up, but found that all food services on the campus were closed on weekends and there was nothing nearby off-campus.

From the outside, the library building seemed large and intimidating. Upon entering, she felt a bit like an intruder. She didn't recognize any of the faces. There were a couple of service desks with staff behind them, but they all seemed preoccupied with something and didn't notice her. It didn't seem appropriate to interrupt them and ask for help. It seemed obvious that she was supposed to figure this out on her own. She was, after all, a university student.

Then she noticed a friend of hers at one of the public workstations. She approached her friend and asked if he could help her. Maria's friend knew a few things about the library. He had been to a library instruction session for his English class, so he knew that reserve materials could be obtained at the circulation desk. Her friend guided her to the second floor of the library where the photocopiers were located. Maria was going to copy the articles so she could read them at home. However, the copiers were all out of paper. Maria and her friend went back to the first floor and told the person at one of the desks about the photocopiers. They said they couldn't do anything about it since photocopiers were maintained by a different department of the university and the library didn't have the keys to open the photocopiers and add paper. Hopefully, the student worker who maintained the copiers would come by soon and address the problem.

The two students then searched the library's catalog for a few articles but found that the library didn't have any articles on Maria's topic. In fact, they concluded that the library didn't seem to have any resources for anthropology at all. They used Google and found links to articles but couldn't access them without making a credit card payment, which Maria didn't want to do. At that point, Maria's friend had to leave to go to his weekend job. Maria stayed to do a bit more research. She decided to look for a few books on history, for her other class, but found the whole process confusing. After 45 minutes of looking in the stacks on the fourth floor for the book, she approached a person at a service desk. But the person said he worked for the Writing Center, not the library, and suggested she go back to the first floor to ask for help. Back on the first floor, the student worker at the circulation desk told her to ask for help at the other desk, the "reference" desk. The man at that desk seemed busy so she didn't want to bother him. Besides, Maria was going to the public library near her house that night and was confident that she could find what she needed there. She needed to leave for home anyway, since she hadn't had any lunch and it was already dinnertime. It was pouring outside now and the wind had picked up. It was a good twenty-minute walk to the train station and it was beginning to get dark.

Of course, Maria is not a real person. She is a conglomerate of the many observed behaviors and reported experiences of Hispanic students at NEIU. Many of her perceptions and actions are similar to those the research teams observed of students at other ERIAL libraries. This returns us to the opening quote of this chapter, which points out that efforts to serve Latino students will generally benefit all students. This isn't to suggest that all students are the same. Our initial research only scratched the surface of the lives of these students, but uncovered enough to indicate some major action steps our library must take to better serve all students.

Likewise, we should also keep in mind that individual Hispanic students at NEIU may not fit this generic profile at all. However, as a library-user model from which we can propose service and facility enhancements, "Maria" is a helpful abstraction. Next, let's put Maria in the context of being a student at NEIU, a federally designated Hispanic-Serving Institution.

BACKGROUND OF NEIU AND HISPANIC-SERVING INSTITUTIONS

NEIU's main campus is located on the far North Side of Chicago. Within a twenty-mile radius of the campus there are dozens of ethnically diverse communities, and it is from these communities that the university draws most of its student body. The university also has a small satellite location called El Centro in the heart of a nearby Latino community as well as a small campus on the South Side of Chicago, the Carruthers Center for Inner City Studies. Finally, the School of Education oversees an educational community resource center in downtown Chicago, called the Chicago Teachers' Center.

The university estimates that there are over forty languages spoken by students on the main campus. The single largest ethnic group is represented by students who self-identify as "Hispanic," making up over 30 percent of the student population. Among the incoming freshman class of 2009, almost 50 percent of the students self-identified as Hispanic. According to the Department of Education, a Hispanic-Serving Institution is defined as an institution of higher education that

(A) is an eligible institution; and
(B) has an enrollment of undergraduate full-time equivalent students that is at least 25 percent Hispanic students at the end of the award year

immediately preceding the date of application (U.S. Department of Education 2010).

In addition, to qualify for the Title V Developing Hispanic-Serving Institutions Program, an institution must assure that at least 50 percent of its Hispanic students are low-income individuals and the institution must have nonprofit status.

GENERAL TRENDS FOUND IN THE NEIU HISPANIC STUDENT TRANSCRIPTS

By fall of 2009 the NEIU team was completing data collection for the ERIAL Project and had begun coding and analyzing the transcripts. Some overall trends for students emerged during our weekly meetings to review this data. At the end of 2009 we reviewed the Hispanic student responses separately and looked for trends from this subgroup in particular.

Personal Relationships

A clear pattern that emerged when interviewing Hispanic students is that those individuals who played a role in assisting them in the process of their research were generally someone with whom they had a clearly defined relationship and knew from previous interactions. Students sought assistance from their instructor, their former high school teacher, a public librarian whom they had received help from before, peers in their class, and/or a sibling. Students rarely asked for help from someone based on their position (e.g., tutor, librarian, instructor, and so forth). In other words, students did not ask strangers for help. Unfortunately, the reference librarian at the information desk is exactly that to most students: a stranger and one whose role they are not quite sure of. This mirrors what one finds in the literature regarding the importance to Latino students of having an authentic relationship with educators:

> The predominantly non-Latino teaching staff sees students as not sufficiently caring about school, while students see teachers as not sufficiently caring for them. Teachers expect students to demonstrate caring about school with an abstract, or aesthetic commitment to ideas

or practices that purportedly leads to achievement. Immigrant and U.S.-born [Latino] youth on the other hand are committed to an authentic form of caring that emphasizes relationships of reciprocity between teachers and students. (Gandara and Contreras 2009, 105)

This observation was confirmed throughout student interviews. One Latino student stated:

> If a workshop is given, make sure that the workshop is informative, but in a fun way. Don't just hand out paper with information and say, "Here, go ahead and do the research on your own." But actually physically show them. That way they can feel comfortable enough with you and then later on during their next visit they'll come back to you and think, "Oh, she's the librarian that helped me, maybe I can ask her a question. Or I can refer my friends to her." And that way it will be more of a community environment instead of just the professional-to-student relationship.

Keywords used by students included *comfortable, community environment, relationship, person-to-person, connection,* and *communication.* The following quote from an NEIU student illustrates why it is important to students to be able to rely on the person who is helping them: the student grades are at stake.

> I think it's better [i.e., face-to-face reference assistance] because I have e-mailed librarians in the past at Chicago Public Libraries and they haven't e-mailed me back right away. So, let's say I have homework due and I need a book on a specific date and if I don't get it then I'm the one getting the grade, the low grade. So I think if it's more of a person-to-person kind of communication it's better, because you get to know the reaction of the person, you know the librarian is patient enough to answer the question. You get to know the librarian personally, so I think it builds the relationship of librarian-to-student, and that way if you ask a question it will be easier for you.

Finally, trust was revealed to be a key element in asking for assistance from a librarian, as is demonstrated by this interview excerpt:

> ANTHROPOLOGIST: So, in general, how do you expect librarians to help students? What's the most significant thing they can do?

LATINO STUDENT: Well, I think the number one, well if I was a librarian myself, I think the number one thing that I would do is try to bring trust to a student . . . because if I was a shy student I would want to work with a librarian who I could trust, who I knew that I could have a connection with.

Family and Geography

The literature on Latino students emphasizes the central role family relationships play in a student's life and the corresponding geographic anchoring that occurs as a result of these family ties.

> In most circles, when I hear common experiences of Latinos described, the role of the family is often the first characteristic mentioned. This occurs so frequently that valuing the family as a characteristic of Latino college students borders on a stereotype. However, . . . family does play an important role in the college experience of Latino students. (Ortiz 2004, 91)

These strong ties and perceived obligations to family members lead many Latino students to live at home with their parents and attend colleges in their local area (Dayton et al. 2004, 33). Leaving home to attend university can be especially challenging to young Latinas and their parents (Gonzalez, Jovel, and Stoner 2004, 19–24). There is also often an expectation to work to help support the family financially (Gandara and Contreras 2009, 191). A common result is that these students are trying to balance work and school, spend significant time commuting, and have limited access to quiet space for studying.

One Latina, who had a GPA of 3.9, stated that family issues take precedence over her academic goals because it is difficult to do well in school if those issues distract her:

> Um, at this point no, [I'm] just focusing on finishing because I've been coming here for seven years already. I've had to take a couple semesters off here and there for personal family reasons. I should have graduated two semesters ago, but it's just whenever something has come up I feel that it's important to take care of that because I think it affects your schoolwork and you're not able to do as well as you

could have done otherwise, so yeah, I believe that, that's important and when I come to school I want to try to do my best.

Although specific data are not available, based on interviews it appears that a high percentage of all NEIU students live at home, perhaps because of the strong familial connection, but certainly due to financial constraints, as this student notes:

> ANTHROPOLOGIST: Would you like to say anything more about challenges and benefits of commuting?
>
> LATINO STUDENT: Well, it helps because you know, we live at home and it's more affordable than living on campus in a dorm or something,

Workshops on Using Library Resources Are Appreciated, Helpful, and Need to Be Increased

Latino students in general responded positively to library workshops, noting how helpful the sessions had been. Many students made strong statements that there should be more library workshops and they should be offered much earlier in students' academic careers. One student commented "I didn't know how to use the NEIU library . . . I'm definitely glad I took the workshop, so I think the one thing that would help the whole student body period would be giving workshops to incoming freshman students." Another student echoed this thought in the following statement: "Well, I like this [library], it has a lot of space and a lot of resources, but I just learned like a month ago how to use the resources and I've been here for like three years. But I didn't know how to do the research." These themes of not knowing how to use the library and wanting more and earlier library workshops were repeated throughout the interviews.

Asking for Help

Although students were appreciative of the workshops they attended, many of the same students expressed a reluctance to ask for help. Here is a conversation that illustrates this in painful detail:

> ANTHROPOLOGIST: Let's see. So, when you went to see the first librarian that you described to me, where you needed help finding ar-

ticles in ERIC or some other database, I'm just going to ask you a list of questions that are related to this. Did you ask for help with interpreting the assignment?

LATINO STUDENT: No.

ANTHROPOLOGIST: Did you need that help?

LATINO STUDENT: Yes.

ANTHROPOLOGIST: Did you ask for help with evaluating resources?

LATINO STUDENT: No.

ANTHROPOLOGIST: Did you need that help?

LATINO STUDENT: Yeah.

ANTHROPOLOGIST: Did you ask for help with identifying appropriate sources?

LATINO STUDENT: Yes.

ANTHROPOLOGIST: Did you ask for help with citing sources?

LATINO STUDENT: No.

ANTHROPOLOGIST: Did you need that help?

LATINO STUDENT: Yeah.

ANTHROPOLOGIST: Did you ask for help with using the card catalog? Or not the card catalog, the [online] catalog?

LATINO STUDENT: No.

ANTHROPOLOGIST: Did you need that help?

LATINO STUDENT: It would help.

ANTHROPOLOGIST: Okay. Did you ask for help using the databases or indexes? You, yes you did. [The student had explained in the earlier part of this interview that he had sought help with using online databases.]

LATINO STUDENT: Yes.

ANTHROPOLOGIST: Did you ask for help locating items on the shelves?

LATINO STUDENT: I didn't ask for help, well I asked him [the librarian] what floor [the item was on], but that's it.

ANTHROPOLOGIST: Okay. Let's see, and did you ask for any help with using computers?

LATINO STUDENT: No.

ANTHROPOLOGIST: Did you need that help?

LATINO STUDENT: Yeah. Yeah.

Perhaps many of the Latino students that attend college are there precisely because they had to be independent and strong enough to make it on their own. The following quote, from a DePaul student interviewed by the ERIAL Project, succinctly illustrates this point:

LATINO STUDENT: I'm not big on asking for help either.

ANTHROPOLOGIST: Oh yeah? Why is that?

LATINO STUDENT: I don't know, I think it's something that comes back from high school—I think my mom wasn't able to help me a lot, so just being in school, like the school I went to, although they said they would help, they weren't very pushy on helping. I felt very independent, that I had to do it on my own. It was kind of transferred onto now.

ANTHROPOLOGIST: You were saying you didn't typically ask your mom for help? Or you couldn't?

LATINO STUDENT: Oh no.

ANTHROPOLOGIST: Okay and why's that?

LATINO STUDENT: My mom emigrated here from Mexico when she was twenty, and she only has like a sixth-grade education.

Several students in this group expressed a personal expectation that they should be able to work independently and not ask for help.

Peer Support and Opinions Are Important

During the course of the ERIAL study we observed a lot of students working together, not just because they had a group project, but because of formal and informal peer mentoring. This has a variety of implications for library space.

> LATINO STUDENT: Definitely work in groups, because I think it's easier when you work with a partner, than . . .alone. Because if you're working by yourself and you spend too much time trying to study and focus but at the same time you get distracted or get bored easily. So, when you do it in groups or in pairs it's easier for you to help each other. Have like a study buddy, basically.

The following student mentions the key role her friends played in supporting her goal to turn in her assignment on time. She also mentions a student peer mentoring program for Latino students, DALE (Developing Academic Leadership through Engagement).

> ANTHROPOLOGIST: So, you say, you went to the writing center twice and you asked an old high school teacher for help?
>
> LATINO STUDENT: Yeah.
>
> ANTHROPOLOGIST: Wow. And you talked to someone from DALE and you talked to your professor.
>
> LATINO STUDENT: Yes.
>
> ANTHROPOLOGIST: Is there anybody else that you talked to about this paper?
>
> LATINO STUDENT: Like two of my friends.
>
> ANTHROPOLOGIST: Oh yeah, what were you talking about with your friends?
>
> LATINO STUDENT: I was giving up on it and they kind of pushed me like no come on you can do this.

ANTHROPOLOGIST: Oh, what was hard about it?

LATINO STUDENT: I was going crazy because the deadline was coming up and then the writing lab wouldn't help much and since I procrastinated a lot I was just going crazy about it. And I was actually going to just not turn it in.

ANTHROPOLOGIST: Oh, you were going to get an incomplete?

LATINO STUDENT: Yeah, but no you know I don't need that. I want A's.

ANTHROPOLOGIST: Gotcha.

LATINO STUDENT: And I got an A at the end, so it was worth it.

The following quote is from a DALE student who used what he learned from the library workshops to help his friends with their work:

I think the library did provide enough structured information because at the workshop I learned a lot. I didn't know how to use the NEIU library before because again I'm a freshman. So, it was my first time doing a research paper at this college. So, at the workshop I learned how to use the Academic Search Premiere and I learned how to look for books and the different levels and how they were alphabetically ordered. So, I didn't know that until I was handed all this paperwork and structured guidelines and everything, especially by the teacher. And so I actually ended up helping a couple of my friends, classmates with their research paper even though I didn't ask them for help . . .
. . . And so I know a lot of my friends do not know how to even use a call number or even what a call number is. So, I think I kind of have the advantage of that.

Students apparently do talk with each other about the quality of library services:

LATINO STUDENT: I've heard issues with different students who had issues with different librarians.

ANTHROPOLOGIST: Oh, yeah?

LATINO STUDENT: Not necessarily at NEIU, but outside at different campuses or public libraries. And so they [students], sometimes they complain. The one thing that most students complain about is the fact that some librarians are not patient.

Librarians Are Not on Many Latino Students' Radars

A striking observation from the study is that many students were unaware of librarians as having relevance to their studies at the university. Moreover, there were several Latino students who did not even seem familiar with the term *librarian.* They referred to the librarian giving an instruction session as "the lady giving the workshop," or the reference librarian as "the man at the desk," or "the lady at the desk." As noted above, some students acknowledged the help that they received from librarians giving workshops, and were quite thankful, but the number of students who were simply unaware of the existence or purpose of librarians is distressing. The most obvious explanation for this, which needs confirmation, is that these students completed their K-12 education without any help from a school librarian. It is quite likely that the schools they attended did not have a librarian, or perhaps even a school library. However, they did use public libraries for satisfying their information needs. In fact, many students at Chicago ERIAL institutions identified the public library as their preferred library even during their college career. They were comfortable there, knew the library staff, and it was a familiar place.

It may be that for these students, an academic library with librarians specifically available to support students' research and study needs is an unfamiliar model. They seemed to have little understanding that the NEIU collections, online resources, and services were different from the public library near their home.

Making Ends Meet Is a Major Focus

In January 2009, the ERIAL librarians convened for an initial two-day hands-on training for conducting ethnographic research. One Latina student, who worked in the NEIU library, volunteered to be interviewed so that appropriate interviewing techniques could be illustrated by the project anthropologists. Many of the librarians present were immediately struck by the content of the interview. They were impressed by the student's perseverance. She had to commute long hours to and from school on public transportation (a pattern we observed with NEIU students), help take care of nephews and nieces and school them in their homework, try to find a quiet place to study at home and, on top of all this, work at the library. It is that last responsibility, trying to work and manage the financial demands of attending college, which may be the most significant issue for NEIU students in general and Latinos specifically.

Retention is generally identified as the biggest issue universities must address for Latino students. And one of the greatest factors affecting retention is the limited financial resources Latinos have for paying for college.

> LIBRARIAN: And you work how many hours?
>
> LATINO STUDENT: I work full time so I work usually 8–10 hours a day.
>
> LIBRARIAN: Then you come home. Do you take evening classes?
>
> LATINO STUDENT: I take evening classes. I work from midnight to 8 in the morning. So at night I'm working, morning I try to sleep a little bit and at night I take classes. I don't have too much time to wander around.

Nevertheless, many Hispanic students are finding it increasingly difficult to earn enough money and obtain enough loans to pay for college, while still meeting the financial needs of their families. In fact, this issue has been identified as the main reason why Hispanic students are unable to finish college (Lopez 2009, 1). Unfortunately, libraries are limited in how well they can help students directly with the financial challenges they face, but they can work to reduce challenges and frustrations that students encounter within the library.

LIBRARIANS CONNECTING TO LATINO STUDENTS

After analyzing local data and working with their resident anthropologist, each ERIAL library created a list of action items to address ways to better support students' research needs. The NEIU team identified 59 action items for consideration. With regard to Hispanic students at NEIU, I would like to highlight four broad areas of focus and how some of these action items address related issues and opportunities.

To begin with, many Latino students who enroll at NEIU start their college career with very little exposure or background to library resources or librarians playing a role in their K-12 education, beyond what they might have found at the public library. To many students, the only obvious difference between their public and university library would be the size. It is not necessarily obvious to these students that the resources and services to help them successfully complete their assignments are quite different.

A second and somewhat related area of focus is that librarians remain strangers to most of these students. Students may be exposed to one-shot instruction sessions and some interactions at the reference desk, but these are brief exchanges. Students simply have little opportunity to become familiar with individual librarians and learn how they can help.

The NEIU team has identified dozens of action items to help address both of these issues. These action items range from short- to long-term and from simple to complex. As examples, I am going to discuss two action items which have long-term strategic implications.

Perhaps the most significant step we have taken to date is to establish a Library Service Center at the El Centro campus. El Centro has approximately 1,000 students and is located about four miles from the main campus, in the heart of one of Chicago's Latino communities. Students at El Centro also take classes at the main campus. El Centro makes it easier for new students to adjust to the initial rigors of college studying and also actively reaches out to the Latino community, offering a variety of services. Until now, students at El Centro were expected to come to the main campus for library services.

In the fall of 2010, we opened a new Library Resource Center on the El Centro campus. By restructuring staffing at some of our service desks in the main library, we are able to staff this facility. But the goal is not to simply act as a branch library. Our intent is to be available for these students on a more intensive level, mentoring them and providing support for their studies. On weekends, we provide special workshops to the Latino community, including the parents and siblings of these students. The library staff that work at El Centro also work at the main library offering reference and instruction services. Library staff can encourage El Centro students to visit them at the main library, providing a supportive introduction to a sometimes intimidating library. We have also hired more Latino students to work in the library and intend to take greater advantage of our Spanish-speaking librarians, of whom we have several. In addition, we have made significant purchases of online materials, in both English and Spanish, to support these students and the Latino community at large.

Another major action item, which will take more time to implement and to see results, is working with high school teachers in the Chicago area to provide high school students a greater awareness of libraries. We have unique opportunities at our disposal. First, our College of Education graduates a large number of the teachers who teach in the Chicago area. So, by working with our College of Education, we hope to raise awareness of these issues and offer practical opportunities for students to utilize some of the numerous academic libraries in the Chicago area. Second, the College of Education supports and administers the Chicago Teacher's Center in Chicago, which works with the community and the teachers in the Chicago area to enhance education. We intend to use this avenue to reach out to educators in Chicago to help them with issues of information literacy.

The third area of focus is on the barriers of effective service and convenience. This is an issue that is a challenge for many libraries, and ours is no exception. We identified numerous action items that fall under this category, but none were uniquely focused on Latino students (e.g., longer library hours, a library café for food on evenings and weekends, better photocopy services, and more computers). It is possible that as we continue our research, additional items will in fact be identified as being a bigger issue for Latino students than for students at large.

The fourth area of focus is on mentoring and support. This is an area of value to all students, however, some of our action items relate specifically to Latino students. As mentioned earlier, this is one of the goals identified in the creation of the El Centro Library Resource Center. However, there are numerous organizations on campus which offer student peer mentoring, some of them specifically for Latino students. Our instruction coordinator, who is bilingual, has offered training sessions to these peer mentoring groups to provide support, as well as to keep them informed of library services they can utilize and suggest to other students.

Many of the identified action items require the library to work with other university departments and offices to bring about the needed changes and improvements. For example, to move forward on many needed building enhancements, we have to work closely with and gain the support of the Facilities Department, University Computing, and the Development Office. One of the most important groups to work with is the teaching faculty. They are obviously a critical constituency with whom the library needs to collaborate. Recognizing that we need to strategically develop and manage our relationships within the university to more effectively achieve our goals, the library has established an Outreach Committee, which will include guidance from professionals with experience in this area of relationship management.

CONCLUSIONS

Hispanic students represent an important and growing population which academic librarians need to learn more about. Since the population that falls under the ethnic description of "Hispanic" or "Latino" is so diverse, it is important for librarians to research the local population that they are serving and not rely on reports of specific populations in other areas, or on reports of the general population at large in North America. Qualitative data on local populations can be gathered by pursuing original ethnographic research. Librarians may be able to obtain important quantitative data from their own Office of Institutional Research, and in the case where more quantitative data is needed, work with their OIR in gathering the additional information.

At NEIU our initial ethnographic research showed that our Hispanic students had very similar needs, issues, and experiences as our student body at large. Pursuing action items that serve our Hispanic students generally also serves all students. We did, however, identify certain action items that targeted Hispanic students specifically. The most significant is the creation of a library facility at the El Centro campus with services that are focused on personal mentoring and support instead of brief reference transactions or one-shot instruction.

We anticipate that our continued pursuit to gather more qualitative and quantitative information on our Hispanic students will lead to continued insights on how the library and librarian can best support their success.

NOTES

1. For a definition of the term *generation 1.5* and a discussion of the general characteristics of that population, see page 246 of Haras' article "(Generation 1.5) Latino Students and the Library: A Case Study."

2. This next phase of our research will seek answers to the following:

- Did the student's forebears immigrate to the United States in the past 100 years and if so, from which country or countries?
- Is the student first-generation, generation 1.5, second-generation or third-generation Latino or other nationality or ethnic group? (See the Pew Hispanic Center's survey brief regarding the definitions and characteristics of these different generations at http://pewhispanic.org/files/factsheets/13.pdf.)
- In which language is the student most comfortable speaking? Reading? Writing?
- Does the student live at home with one or both parents?
- Which language are the student's parent(s) most comfortable speaking? Reading? Writing?
- What is the educational level of the student's parents?
- Is the student working full time? Part time?
- How is the student financing his or her education?
- What kind of transportation does the student have available for commuting to school?
- How long does it take for the student to commute to school?
- Does the student have ready access to a computer at home? At work?
- If the student has computer access, does he or she have adequate Internet access?
- Does the student's high school have a library? Does the library have adequate resources to support the high school curriculum and research needs of the high school students?

There are many other areas we would like to explore in more detail regarding the students' backgrounds and environments. These all have implications for the library's space, services, fees, methods of communication, and so on.

7

First-Generation College Students: A Sketch of Their Research Process

FIROUZEH LOGAN AND
ELIZABETH PICKARD

The ERIAL research team at the University of Illinois at Chicago focused on the research process of first-year, first-generation college students. As the three Chicago-area ERIAL project teams began assembling information for the Library Services and Technology Act grant application, the different demographic profiles of the universities (see chapter 1) began to suggest potential areas of research. UIC is a state-funded public research institution located in the near West Side of Chicago and serves approximately 27,000 students. The stated mission of UIC is to provide "the broadest access to the highest levels of intellectual excellence" (UIC Faculty Senate). This mission includes two key goals that influenced the library's decision to participate in the ERIAL Project and also helped single out the population on which the UIC's research would focus: (1) to provide a wide range of students with the educational opportunity only a leading research university can offer, and (2) to foster scholarship and practices that reflect and respond to the increasing diversity of the United States in a rapidly globalizing world.

The ERIAL Project team at UIC was particularly interested in examining library services to individuals of diverse geographic, cultural, and socioeconomic backgrounds because according to UIC's enrollment data, UIC has an extremely diverse student body (UIC Office of Institutional Research, 2010). Furthermore, first-generation college students constitute a large portion of this population (UIC Office of the Vice Chancellor 2002), making them a natural choice for the focus of this project.

The ERIAL Project at UIC allowed the library to paint a rich portrait of the first-year, first-generation college students and to learn details of what they actually do when they are assigned a research project. It also allowed the examination of student needs from the students' perspective. With these insights, the library plans to tailor its services to address first-generation students' unique needs and to help bridge their perceived academic achievement gap in learning and producing scholarly work.

BACKGROUND

Ethnography's capacity to create a sense of "being there" (Geertz 1988, 16) makes the ethnographic approach particularly useful for this study, and ethnography has become increasingly used and valued as a methodology in library studies (see chapter 1). In his review of the University of Rochester Library's ethnographic study, *Studying Students: The Undergraduate Research Project* (Foster and Gibbons 2007), Michael Seadle (2007) called for the increased use of ethnography as a way of understanding libraries. In support of using ethnography to analyze library services, Michelynn McKnight (2001) reviewed studies of information-seeking behavior and found a consistent discrepancy between what subjects report on surveys and what they actually do when seeking information. Ethnography can, therein, present a more complete and accurate picture of a group under study.

Prior studies have also utilized ethnographic approaches such as interviewing to examine library use by first-generation students. "Make the Numbers Count" interviewed college students at the University of the Arts London about their experience using the library (Conway et al. 2009). Similarly, "(Generation 1.5) Latino Students in the Library" used a combination of interviewing and surveys to examine library usage among Latino students at California State University, Los Angeles (Haras et al. 2008), while "Library Service for the First-Generation College Student" used surveys and interviews to explore the library experience and skills of first-generation college students at California State University, Fresno (Tyckoson 2000). Like McKnight, Tyckoson also found that interview results illuminated and altered the interpretation of survey results. The findings of all three studies showed that first-generation students are likely to have more difficulties facing the challenges of university-level research than their peers, and that these difficulties are worth exploring in more depth in order to develop and revise services to help address these concerns. These challenges include, but are not confined to, limited technology and information literacy skills and a lack of familiarity with the research process.

UIC has a large first-generation student population and has commissioned two studies over the last ten years to better understand these students and help them meet the challenges they face as new undergraduates. The most recent study examined Chicago Public School (CPS) high school graduates attending UIC. UIC is the number-one recipient of CPS graduates who attend four-year colleges or universities. Of the 3,182 students in the 2009 freshman class who participated in the entering student survey, 708 were CPS students. This study found that just over one-half of the CPS students surveyed in 2009 had no exposure to college from their parents, and found that "generally, UIC students report that English is not their first language at a higher rate than their peers at other four year universities across the country" (UIC Office of the Vice Provost for Academic and Enrollment Services and UIC Office of the Vice Chancellor for Student Affairs 2009). A second UIC study, entitled "Who Are the First-Generation Students at UIC," examined the difference between first-generation college students and students with college-educated parents (UIC Office of the Vice Chancellor 2002). It states: "The difference in ACT scores between these two groups suggests that first-generation students may be at a disadvantage from the moment they enter college. Though this information contributes to our understanding of the UIC first-generation population, by no means does it offer a complete picture. There is much more to learn about these students and what services and resources we need to provide to ensure that they meet their academic goals."

In order to help complete the picture, the ERIAL Project UIC team included first-generation students from many ethnic backgrounds and employed ethnographic methods to explore not just perceptions and use of the university library, but also students' research process and practices as a whole.

METHODOLOGY

One of the primary purposes of the ERIAL project at UIC was to explore conclusions drawn from prior studies to further target ways in which academic librarians might address first-generation college patrons' potential skills gaps. The use of ethnography was intended to help illuminate the nuances present in students' understanding of the research process and the librarian's role, and thus to help identify ways of potentially expanding and honing that role.

For the UIC analysis, the authors reviewed the results of thirty-three student interviews collected during the ERIAL Project. The UIC interview protocol specifically asked student participants if they were the first members of their families to attend college, either in the United States or elsewhere.[1] The UIC research team wanted to specifically examine the research experience of first-year students and identify these students' expectations of libraries before they developed UIC-specific research habits. Of the 33 students interviewed, 32 self-identified as first-year students, and of these, 18 self-identified as first-generation college students. The results of these 18 interviews provide the data analyzed in this chapter.

In order to get a general sense of participants' academic interests and family background, they were asked several questions. In terms of family background, students were asked "Did your parents or grandparents attend college?" and "What language do you speak at home?" Of the 18 first-generation students interviewed, only 9 reported English was the language spoken at home. The other 9 mentioned English in conjunction with Spanish, Polish, Punjabi, Tibetan, Korean, Cantonese, and Chinese. Thus, the UIC ERIAL team sample very closely mirrors the UIC campus as a whole, as reported by the Office of the Vice Provost for Academic and Enrollment Services, Office of the Vice Chancellor for Student Affairs.

Participants also represented a wide range of majors, the most popular of which were psychology (three students) and biology (two students).

Three participants were double majors, focusing on creative writing and economics, history and political science, and Polish and Spanish economics. One participant was undecided, and the rest of the majors included anthropology, computer science, criminal justice, education, English, entrepreneurship, kinesiology, mathematics, and Russian sociology.

RESEARCH EXPERIENCE BEFORE COLLEGE

The UIC team wanted to explore not only students' previous exposure to college and questions of native language, but also their educational history and their knowledge of the information universe as well as where they acquired this knowledge. According to UIC's 2009 survey, students graduate from all kinds of schools: non-Chicago public high schools, Chicago public schools, and Cook and adjacent county schools (Office of the Vice Provost for Academic and Enrollment Services and Office of the Vice Chancellor for Student Affairs 2009).[2] The targeted ERIAL sample had equally varied high school experiences. They named schools such as Illinois Math and Science Academy, a recognized leading college preparatory school in math and education (Gamerman et al. 2007), Whitney Young, a magnet college prep school, Lane Technical, and other unnamed public and private schools.

Anecdotally, UIC librarians and faculty seem to suspect that first-year students are fairly naive about the complexity of information and the research process. This project revealed, however, that all of the students interviewed had, in fact, conducted a research project in high school. Of course, not all research projects are created equally, and even though some of these students may need help in learning how to search for and retrieve information, they did seem to recognize the need for quality information.

Participants were asked, "Did you write a long research paper or work on a large research project before attending college?" In describing the resources they used in high school, the students used language that ranged from simple to that of an experienced researcher. Some spoke generically of "online" sources, but others spoke of specific research tools. Some had been allowed to use Wikipedia, but most had not. However, in describing their sources, most used very standard academic terminology: "literary and scientific journals," "primary source documents," "peer-reviewed journals." These students clearly knew to look for quality information.

SEARCHING

To understand students' approaches to finding information, participants were asked, "How did you search for information sources for this project?" or "Did you search online?" "Did you use print materials? And "How did you choose what you used?" Seventeen participants discussed where they searched for sources. Participants sometimes spoke of resources they used to find information (such as search engines, databases, or catalogs) interchangeably with sources containing the information itself, such as journal articles or books, and they drew a general picture about their use of library and nonlibrary resources, as well as their preference for online versus print format.

All seventeen participants searched online for sources. "Online" searching seemed to mean different things to different participants, and they used online resources to reach a variety of goals. Some participants spoke of online searching in a very general sense and did not specify where they looked. Eight participants made some mention of searching "online" or using the "Internet" or a "website" without mentioning Google specifically or referencing the library or any identifiable library resources. Other participants used one of Google's many services. Nine of the participants used Google at some point during their search and two used Google Scholar as well. Four participants used Google to do preliminary searching on a topic, "just to see what was out there," and two used it to get "background" information. Another two students used Google and Google Scholar to find and access articles, while one student used Google to find a book preview (potentially via Google Books) to get the content of a book to quote and cite instead of locating the entire book. The remaining two students used Google and Google Scholar but did not specify to what purpose. The students that used Google Scholar noted that they had learned about this resource during a library instruction session. In general, participants seemed to have a sense that some sources were more reliable than others. Most of them used Google only for preliminary searching and "not to quote." One participant stated directly, " I used Google just to bounce ideas around. It wasn't, necessarily, like a way to, like, research . . . I would never quote Wikipedia or anything." This participant was the only one to mention Wikipedia.

Of the participants who used online library resources, some explicitly stated understanding that the library context offered more authority, but often without an acknowledgment or apparent awareness that the resources they were using came from the library. Eleven participants used online library resources such as the journal article databases and/or the library catalog, but only seven explicitly differentiated library and non-library sources when using both types in conjunction. Two participants used both library and nonlibrary online resources, but did not seem to be aware that "JSTOR.com" was a library resource. While speaking about JSTOR, one later observed, "But all the books I got were from the library." Two participants explained that they focused entirely on library resources. One stated, "I used the online catalog search engine thing . . . So, it was easier to find reliable sources I could use." Two participants noted that they did not use the library at all. One used his high school website, and the other "just looked online." When asked, both stated they did not know the UIC Library had databases that could search scholarly sources relevant to their topics.

The prompting question, "Did you use print materials?" attempted to obtain information specifically about participants' use of print indices, but was often interpreted by both interviewer and participant as asking about selecting sources in print format such as journal articles and books. As a result, the responses were mixed but gave an idea of whether the partici-pants used articles and books more frequently in online or in print form. Several participants used print books, but it was unclear whether or not the instructor had required the use of books. One stated, "I was able to find a lot of information in the books that I had and just a few supplemental facts on websites." Two participants mentioned browsing the shelves for additional books. One explained, "I went to the architecture section and found a whole shelf of Sears Tower." None indicated that they used print journal articles. One participant seemed to think using print sources was more difficult, stating that, after this initial research project, the participant felt "prepared now" to use print sources. In general, responses were quite suggestive of the fact that more participants used and preferred online sources to print sources. Whether they felt this way about both articles and books or just about articles was not clear.

Of the eighteen participants who were asked why they used online resources, all indicated that they perceived online resources as easier to use. Their responses ranged from "electronic was just easier" and online searching was "most convenient" to more specific explanations, such as "out of all the things I used, Google Scholar was probably the easiest, so I just used that one" and "I didn't have to go to the library to pick something up, like the articles were there." The situation, described above, in which the participant used an online preview of a book rather than getting the physical object, is fairly suggestive that convenience is a priority as well. It is not clear whether "easier" in the participants' responses referred to the act of searching for sources or physically accessing the sources. Likewise, it would be illuminating to further parse the word "online."

SOURCE SELECTION: NUMBER

Participants were asked, "How did you know when you had enough sources?" Thirteen participants discussed their methods of determining when they had enough sources to complete their research projects. Analysis of the thirteen responses revealed four main approaches: using the number set by their instructors, using a number adequate (as determined by the student) to meet the page length set by their instructors, using a number adequate to support their topics, or some mixture of the three. The majority of students negotiated the instructors' parameters and the need for information to support their topics rather than sticking wholly to one or the other. Instructors' parameters varied in terms of the number of sources required or allowed as well as the page length required for the assignment. Some instructors set only a minimum number of sources, while others set an exact number or a range of numbers of sources that students were required and allowed to have.

Instructors specified an exact number of sources for two participants who did not indicate whether or not they would have done more if allowed. Only one participant stuck to the minimum number of sources required by his instructors, explaining that he had tried to do the minimum but had also tried to cover the topic.

Four participants were given a range in the number of sources required, and all four met the maximum number allowed by the instructor. All of these students also explained that they would have used more sources if allowed. However, participants experienced the maximum limit differently. One felt he was willing to go beyond the page length, but the instructor explained that writers must learn to be concise. Another felt, because he was only allowed eight sources, that he wasted a lot of time trying to find all the information in a few sources when he had already found a larger number of relevant sources to cover the topic. He explained, "I had already exceeded the eight . . . You need a certain amount of information in order to fully write your paper, and even with eight sources, I didn't have enough, and so I had to keep looking for more information—the right kind of sources." Still another found permission in the maximum to cut out the "tedious to read" sources. Although most of these students expressed a clear desire to use enough sources to satisfactorily support their topics, for all of them, the instructors' parameters were the defining criteria for determining the final number of sources to include in their projects.

Likewise, three participants selected the number of sources according to the page-length requirements of their instructors, but still with the goal of thoroughly addressing their topics. One stated, "I knew I had enough sources when I was confident about my thesis statement, and I felt like I could actually write five to six pages on it," while another explained, "I think I had more than I needed, but I just wanted to make sure it would be a long paper." A third actually determined the number of points he made in order to fit the page-length and still adequately support those points. He stated, "Once I had at least two sources on it [a main point], I would stop there and move on to the next, because the paper was limited to eight pages." An idea common to all three cases is that the students aimed for enough sources to write the required page-length parameter, but also that "enough" suggests the idea of adequately supporting their topics for that length.

Finally, three participants clearly prioritized covering the topic above other approaches. Two of them knowingly exceeded the instructors' set maximum number of sources in order to support their topics to the degree they felt was adequate. One explained in reference to the six-source maximum set by the instructor, "I think I used eight . . . Sometimes the information that you get from a source—it's not enough." The other stated, "I knew I needed four, but I went ahead and used, probably six . . . Once I had that [the topic] covered, I knew that was enough." The third did not mention the instructor's parameters and spoke only of selecting sources appropriate to cover the topic.

In essence, the instructors' parameters seemed to be the top priority in determining how many sources to use, but adequately covering the topic was a very close second. Of the thirteen participants that discussed choosing sources, all of them acknowledged their instructors' parameters and all but two worked within them. All but two participants, who did not discuss whether or not they took covering the topic into account, discussed wanting to cover the topic thoroughly and/or wanting to have found and used more than the maximum allowed number of sources.

SOURCE SELECTION: TYPE

Participants were asked, "How did you know when you had the right kind of sources?" Fifteen participants discussed evaluating sources to determine which were most appropriate for their research projects. Most participants found more than the required number of sources and narrowed their selection to those they used in their bibliographies. One participant's professor assigned some of the sources he used. However, the sources participants themselves selected were chosen according to three main criteria: the source's relevance to the research topic, scholarly appearance, and the participant's ability to understand the information.

Relevance

Relevance to the research topic was a criterion common to all participants' selections. Most participants spoke of relevance as if it was an assumed criterion, but eight gave specific details about what relevance means to them. Three stated the obvious, such as, "They were talking about the same thing I was." Others discussed selecting sources based on the amount or quality of information they contained. One participant explained he chose sources based on "the amount of information I was able to pull from them," and another went on to say, "I read through them and saw which information was relevant . . . the ones that had either the most information or the interesting facts were the ones I chose." Two others tried to balance pros and cons, and described the process saying, "They [the sources] were useful. I used them for my argument and for my counter-argument," and "I would first see if it was relevant to my topic. I kind of tried to have an equal amount of sources that agreed—that I agreed with—and then disagreed with . . . so that way the professor could see I was trying to see both sides of the story." One participant kept relevance in mind but was caught up in learning about the topic. He stated, "Some of them were much harder to narrow down, because I get so engrossed in the topic, I don't realize if it's relevant or not to my paper."

Scholarly

Six participants described evaluating sources to determine whether or not they were scholarly as part of their selection process. Not all used the term *scholarly*. Some spoke of peer-reviewed and reliable sources as well. Some participants spoke only of evaluating websites, which they did based on terms someone else had established for them, but did not explain who. One stated that "I just know not to trust websites that end in .com," and the other explained, "I know they wouldn't accept Wikipedia for sure, but everything I was on, I think, was mostly government or news organizations." Two of the participants that discussed books and articles used the context in which they found the sources as scholarly signifiers. Another used the fact that he found it "on the UIC website" as a signifier that the source was "reliable." Another determined that sources were scholarly because the database told him so. He explained, "I made sure they were peer-reviewed . . . it [the database] says it on there . . . in PsycINFO it says like how many people used the article or journal, so we went off of that as well. It's like the more it's used, it was like better information." This participant also had some understanding of how to evaluate the sources himself, clearly, in that he was able to explain citation reporting. Two participants looked at the sources themselves for signifiers. One participant chose sources that were "written by professors," and another looked at visual cues and the ease with which he could understand the information the sources provided. He explained, "Okay, this has to be scholarly, because it looks, I guess, fancy . . . it wasn't big print . . . no pictures . . . If it's difficult to read, then you know it has to be scholarly."

Comprehensible

Three participants discussed the ease with which they understood the source's information as a factor in selecting, or not selecting, that source. As noted above, one participant used the fact that a source was difficult for him to understand as a signifier that it was scholarly and so selected it to use. However, two other participants rejected sources they had trouble understanding. One explained, "When I found something that's part of my interests, something I feel like I had a good understanding of, comprehension of, I was able to start the project." The other stated, "Sources I don't understand, I just left alone and found something else."

OBSTACLES

Participants were asked, "Were there any other problems or obstacles that you encountered while working on the assignment?" Four students said the library was too big, and people can get lost in the building, indicating that it is very important to ensure students can get help finding materials. Six continued to use the libraries they used in high school because those libraries were familiar to them. Some used the UIC Library, but they also continued to use the more familiar, less intimidating libraries where they went to get help in high school. One participant explained, "At UIC, it's like so big. There's so many students. They [the librarians] are not going to walk around and ask if you need help." Another said, "I get confused just looking at all those books. I don't know what they're for."

Thirteen of the eighteen students spoke about challenges they faced finding sources. Some said they found no sources on their topic; others said there were not enough sources on their topics; some found the information on their topic to be incorrect. A few felt they did not have enough time, and one was bored and could not stay committed. However, most intimated that they did well on their assignment. It would seem these responses were contradictory, yet it is unclear which point in the research process participants were discussing. It seems implicit to their collective response that the obstacles were not permanent. Students seemed to have overcome these obstacles, potentially with some assistance, as was indicated in response to this question and in questions about selecting sources (see above).

GETTING HELP

Participants sought many different types of help with their research projects and sought this help from a variety of people. Participants were asked, with respect to their college research projects, "Did you ask anyone for help?" Sixteen participants discussed seeking help with their projects. Of those, three did not ask for help, and thirteen sought help from people affiliated with the university and/or from people involved in their personal lives. Participants visited some of these people of their own volition and others because it was required or recommended by the instructor.

Participants sought help most often from individuals affiliated directly with their courses. As shown in table 7.1, participants sought help most frequently from their instructors and teaching assistants (TAs). Some participants noted their meetings with instructors were a required part of the course, although most suggested they voluntarily sought help from their instructor or TA after class. Participants sought help from friends and classmates as well. However, participants sought out other university resources such as librarians and the writing center most often after some urging or direct referral. Of the university resources, participants sought help from librarians most frequently after their instructor or TA. All four participants who asked a librarian for help had prior experience in a library, and most

TABLE 7.1 *Seeking Help by Person (in order of popularity)*

From Whom	By Number of Participants	Under What Circumstances	Type of Help
Instructor/TA	10	Mandated, Volunteered	Progress check, proofreading, topic selection, topic honing, where to search for sources, approval of sources, selecting content, organizing project
Friend(s)/ Classmate(s)	9	Volunteered	Proofreading, search terms, how to use databases and/ or catalog, where to search for sources, selecting content, organizing project
Librarian	4	Volunteered	Physically getting to sources, search terms, how to use databases and/or catalog
Family Member(s)	3	Volunteered	Where to search for sources, selecting content, organizing project
Writing Center	1	Referred	Selecting content, organizing project

had some previous exposure to the UIC Library. One participant had not had a library instruction or orientation session and drew a parallel with experience at a public library. The participant stated, "I've done that at the public library, so I figured I could do it here." Two others had had a library instruction session at UIC in which they indicated they were encouraged to seek out the help of a librarian. Likewise, two participants, one of whom had also had a library instruction session, had an orientation session their freshman year during which they were encouraged to ask a librarian for help. Only one participant made use of the Writing Center, and the course instructor had required that visit.

Participants turned to their instructors and TAs for most types of help, as indicated in table 7.1, but they also sought these types of help from other people as well. In contrast, some types of help were unique to certain people. Participants sought help with topics, progress checks, and approval of sources only from their instructors and TAs. Participants sought help physically finding sources only from librarians. Likewise, participants asked librarians, not instructors or TAs, for help using library resources such as the catalog and journal article databases.

The difference in use of university resources and participants' description of when they used specific resources suggests that the built-in nature of students' relationship with their instructors and TAs might be a root cause. Students see their instructors and TAs on a regular basis in class. Convenience and familiarity are fundamental aspects of this built-in relationship. It could be more convenient time-wise to see the instructor or TA just after class rather than make an extra trip to the library. Likewise, the instructor and TA are known quantities to students. Students learn how to communicate with them as part of being in the class. Furthermore, the instructor and TA assign the projects and grade them, thus their suggestions about approaches to the research process probably seem fundamentally trustworthy to their students. Learning where the library is, how to use its services and resources, and determining whether it is a trustworthy place to seek help all take time and effort for students. That being said, the first-generation students that made use of librarians turned to librarians for help using the resources even without a built-in relationship. This combination suggests that lack of awareness of library offerings and their intrinsic value, as well as lack of convenience, may account for the relatively low use of librarians among these first-generation students.

Although additional research needs to be conducted with respect to the reasons students turn to instructors and TAs rather than librarians for help with library resources, a pattern seems to have emerged. In order to draw students to the experts (librarians) that best know what the library offers and how to use it, libraries need to find ways to enhance students' awareness of library resources and services, thus increasing the likelihood that students will value librarians and their expertise enough to seek help from the library.

COMMUNICATION

Every student interviewed owned a cell phone. When asked how they preferred to communicate in general, twelve preferred calling, four preferred instant message or texting, three preferred e-mail, and three preferred face-to-face interactions. However, when asked how they would prefer to work with librarians, all eighteen of the students said they preferred to get help face-to-face. Each expressed their preference in a slightly different way, but their reasons were well-considered: "I can clarify what I'm saying if I need to," "I actually want to be led around the library," and " a phone call is a bit rushed and then sometimes you can't hear the person."

In answer to the question, "Could the library have done anything differently?" one student thought the library had done a "fantastic job" and they were "nice," but they should wear badges or name tags so they would be easier to find. Another thought it was good that librarians did not assume the student had any prior knowledge. It seemed important that librarians not be judgmental. For the most part, the students did not think of librarians as academics, and perhaps would not think to approach them for help, but they thought it very important that librarians smile and act friendly. This is consistent with other studies, such as Jo Bell Whitlatch's (2001) "Evaluating Reference Services," that discuss reference assessment.

CONCLUSIONS

In summary, the ERIAL Project at UIC brought to light some details of how first-generation students conduct their research process. The study demonstrated that first-generation UIC students have a range of experiences and understanding of the research process. In terms of searching for sources, students are willing to use both print and online resources, but online sources were seen as easier to use. The terms *easier* and *online* bear further exploration. In selecting sources, participants chose sources that were relevant to the topic, scholarly, and comprehensible. The instructor's parameters were the defining ones in terms of number, but students were willing to exceed this number in order to adequately cover the topic and sometimes had difficulty paring down to the required limit.

In addition to challenges in finding enough relevant sources in order to adequately address the topic within the maximum allowed, participants had difficulty navigating the physical library. For this they turned solely to librarians for assistance. They also looked to librarians for help using the library's databases and catalog, as well as figuring out search terms. However, they primarily turned to their instructors and TAs for all kinds of help, including areas in which librarians could be the most useful. This omission of librarians could have occurred for many reasons having to do with familiarity, convenience, and the final say of the instructors with whom the students have a mandatory, built-in relationship. The UIC Library and librarians therefore need to seek out ways to increase students' awareness of their services. They also need to find ways to demonstrate the value of their services and of librarians' expertise, so that students are able and willing to seek the best help during the research process. Furthermore, the assessment and design of new reference services should factor in students' preference for a polite, welcoming demeanor and face-to-face encounters with librarians, in conjunction with the ease of online access.

As a result of the ERIAL study, the UIC Library is in the process of implementing changes to its services. In order to make the university library more familiar, convenient, and less intimidating, the library is once again becoming involved in orientation for new students and for new faculty. The hope is to increase students' understanding of the library before they begin setting their research habits. Instruction sessions will emphasize the difference between high school, public, and academic libraries to make the value of academic collections and the services academic librarians offer more apparent. Likewise, the library plans to offer movies and book talks to help make the library a familiar space. The library is also prioritizing outreach to faculty to better ensure that they know and value the library's holdings and services, and thus might be more likely to refer students when appropriate.

The UIC Library is also pursuing additional research in response to the ERIAL Project. In order to better understand the full experience of first-generation students at UIC, a research project using ethnographic methods is under way to explore how first-generation seniors conduct research and to better understand their expectations of librarians, faculty, and themselves during the process. This study will also seek to identify differences between first-generation college students in their first year and senior year to learn how, and if, students develop their research skills over time in college. This research and the data yet to be analyzed from the ERIAL Project will undoubtedly continue to help the UIC Library improve services to first-generation students and the student body as a whole for years to come.

NOTES

1. The research teams for other ERIAL institutions did not explicitly collect this information.

2. Cook and adjacent counties comprise the greater Chicago metropolitan area.

8

Seeing Ourselves As Others See Us: Library Spaces through Student Eyes

JANE TREADWELL, AMANDA BINDER,
AND NATALIE TAGGE

G oing into the twenty-first century, a new model emerged for new and redesigned library spaces in academic libraries. The central service floor, once devoted to the reference desk, the reference collection, the circulation desk, and an area for patron seating, either at tables or computer carrels, gave way to what became known as the "information commons." As more and more library information became electronic (especially the kind of information found in abstracts, indexes, encyclopedias, and other reference sources), much of the reference collection was either weeded or relocated to the circulating collection, and the "footprint" formerly devoted to the collection was turned over to patron seating, frequently configured as computer carrels for three or four people. Tables without computers were also wired for both electricity and data so that students can use their own laptops at them. In addition to the library catalog and databases to which the library subscribed, productivity software, such as the Microsoft Office suite, was loaded onto the computers, transforming them from the "terminals" that were placed in libraries during the three preceding decades for access primarily to the library's online catalog, to workstations at which students can do research, write papers, and if they so choose, surf the Internet or even play games. In addition, the new or renovated library provides a number of collaborative study rooms, both large and small, to accommodate students working in groups. This collaborative work might also extend to the students seated in the information commons itself, with the result that the library—or at least, its main service floor—can no longer be considered a place for quiet study.

Much has been written about the information commons, and some later authors, notably Scott Bennett (2007a, 2007b, 2008, 2009), have refocused the definition so that the emphasis is placed on the student learner rather than the technology that he or she is using, with the resulting name change of "learning commons." A recent book by Forrest and Halbert, *A Field Guide to the Information Commons* (2009), is a good place to start for an overview, and includes contributions by both librarians and architects, as well as a time line of information commons developments. The authors observe, "Technology has enabled new forms of information-seeking behavior . . . causing a revolution in libraries that revisits the idea of the 'commons'—a public place that is free to be used by everyone." For in-depth research undertaken just as the information commons approach was taking hold, Shill and Tonner offer two articles in *College & Research Libraries:* "Creating a Better Place: Physical Improvements in Academic Libraries, 1995–2002" (2003) and "Does the Building Still Matter?" (2004).

Probably no other architectural firm was more responsible for introducing the information commons into American academic libraries than the venerable Boston firm of Shepley, Bulfinch, Richardson, and Abbott (SBRA). Starting with the University of Southern California, and including libraries at Emory, Duke, Marquette, and the ERIAL Project's own Illinois Wesleyan University, they helped to transform the main service floor of many academic libraries into a place brimming with technology and buzzing with activity. However, in a 2005 white paper for the Council on Library and Information Resources, *The Library as Place: Changes in Learning Patterns, Collections, Technology, and Use,* Geoffrey T. Freeman of SBRA notes that "while students are intensely engaged in using new technologies, they also want to enjoy the library as a contemplative oasis" (Freeman 2005, 6). Moreover, Freeman asserts that in planning for a new or renovated library building, the planning team must ground the process in the mission, goals, and values of the institution, and not simply follow the popular template of the time.

BACKGROUND: UNIVERSITY OF ILLINOIS SPRINGFIELD

The University of Illinois Springfield is the small liberal arts campus of the University of Illinois. Founded in 1970, it was for much of its history Sangamon State University, an upper-division university whose student body consisted almost entirely of commuter students. In 2001, the institution began admitting freshmen and now enrolls around 300 per year, increasing the on-campus population to around 1,000 students out of a total of 4,800. Two dormitories, a recreation center, and a new classroom building have been constructed since 2001, giving the campus a much more residential feel. In addition to the residential student population, almost one-quarter of UIS students are in online-only degree programs. Also, a sizable number of students continue to commute to campus. The library thus faces the challenge of serving these three distinct groups of students: residential, online, and commuter.

The Norris L. Brookens Library, constructed in 1975, was the first permanent building on the UIS campus. Constructed in the brutalist style, the Brookens building nevertheless has a futurist heart—it lacks any right angles. The library occupies four floors: a main floor (Level 2), opening to the university quad, two upper floors (Levels 3 and 4), housing the bulk of the library's collections, and a lower level occupied by a café and computer lab. See figure 8.1.

Despite its design, by the beginning of the twenty-first century the building was beginning to show its age, as the original carpets and furnishings were in place in most parts of the building, and where they had been replaced, there was no thought to aesthetic consistency. Because the building had been subdivided down the middle on Levels 2 and 3, when the intent had been for an open floor plan, problems with heating, ventilation, and air conditioning were worse than in most library buildings. The single-paned windows were a disaster from an energy-efficiency viewpoint

FIGURE 8.1 *The exterior of the Brookens Library*

(and had to be replaced for safety reasons just as planning for a renovation was getting under way), the lighting was dreadful, and acoustic separation, especially on the main floor, was nonexistent. One student, commenting on the space in a 2007 LibQual + survey, said that being in the library was "like being in a warehouse or dungeon."

Over the years, numerous studies have been conducted of the Brookens Library building. Two studies conducted in 2003 and 2005 both recommended that the building be renovated. The 2005 study also included plans for a library café, which was built in 2008. The university committed to a renovation master plan after a 2008 study documented that fully half of the deferred maintenance for the entire UIS campus was associated with the Brookens facility. It was determined that work of the magnitude suggested by the deferred maintenance study (involving heating and cooling systems, lighting, windows, and virtually all furnishings) could not be completed piecemeal. To implement all of the necessary improvements identified, a full renovation of the library would be required.

While large structural improvements had to wait, the library did begin to work on some of the recommendations from the two preliminary studies that addressed service quality. In particular, we began the transition from the traditional academic library main service floor to an information commons, reducing the size of the reference collection to make room for more seating, especially more computer seating. We also combined the reference and circulation desks into a single information desk.

Because of these changes to the physical space and library services, as well as the rapid changes in collection development policies (with increased reliance on e-resources), we decided to survey our users and find out how they thought the library was meeting their needs. Thus, we chose to participate in LibQual+, a nationally normed survey that had been developed at Texas A&M University and standardized by the Association of Research Libraries. We participated in the spring of 2007. The data from the survey was rich, giving us much to consider in the way of improvements. In analyzing the results, we discovered an existing area of disparity between the undergraduate and graduate student perceptions of "library as place." Graduate students scored two areas of the library at below the desired minimum level: "library space that inspires study and learning," and "a gateway for study, learning or research."[1] While undergraduates did not rate any areas as below the minimum level, they, too, expressed some concern about "library space that inspires study and learning." However, one area that undergraduates found to be close to the desired level was "community space for group learning and group study." This may have reflected the greater importance of group work in undergraduate education.

Going into the ERIAL project, UIS was determined to look more closely at the difference that the LibQual+ study seemed to suggest between the perceptions of undergraduate and graduate students regarding the library as place. Our hypothesis was that undergraduate students had no problem with the noisy world of the information commons on the main level of the building, while graduate students gravitated more to the quiet study areas on levels three and four. Additionally, we presumed that an age difference was at play: that the more traditionally aged (18–22 years) students would be less likely to seek out quiet study areas and more apt to engage in group study than their older counterparts, who were often returning to college after an absence of some years and had a more traditional notion of what the library should be. These older returning students, we believed, were the ones who were likely to be most dissatisfied with the library building.

In the fall of 2008, the Chicago architectural firm Holabird & Root was selected to develop a master plan for the renovation of the Brookens Library. Over the course of the 2008–2009 academic year, Holabird &

Root architects worked with a Library Design Committee made up of representatives from the library and other stakeholders housed in the Brookens Library building (including the Educational Technology Division of Information Technology Services, the Center for Teaching and Learning, and the College of Education and Human Services) to develop a plan for the building to transform it into a twenty-first-century learning center. The design that emerged features an entry level that brings together librarians, information technologists, the Center for Teaching and Learning, and the Center for First Year Students to form a "success center" focused on student learning. To achieve all of the programming goals for the library, the plan includes an addition that gives the building a more open and light-filled ambience. The building's learning commons is on two levels connected by a very visible grand stairway. To correct the pronounced way-finding difficulties of the Brookens facility, a strong central corridor is also introduced. The design features numerous group study rooms and quiet study areas, as well.

In the course of developing the design program, the architects held a number of visioning sessions with library stakeholders, including two design charrettes (intense focus groups about the existing library and ideas for the future building) with students. Each charrette attracted about five students, most of whom were undergraduates. From these discussions, the following issues with the existing library emerged: way-finding and the maze-like layout of the building, uncomfortable and dated furniture, parts of the stacks that seem cold and even "creepy," lack of acoustical separation, and an overall feeling that the building is not welcoming and attractive. Things students liked about the building included the coffee shop, the lounges, some of the study spaces in the stacks, and the ubiquity of computers throughout the building. Looking to the future, students wanted to see a more open and inviting space, more group study rooms, spaces clearly marked for group study, noise, and socializing, and clearer organization and way-finding. Out of one group came the desire for "both high tech and books together," while another said "be sure to keep part of the library with quiet academic atmosphere, surrounded by books." One of the most intriguing ideas, which affirmed a direction that the design committee was taking, was that "everything geared to studying should be in the library."

AN ETHNOGRAPHIC APPROACH TO LEARNING ABOUT STUDENT PREFERENCES FOR LIBRARY SPACE

Viewing ourselves through the eyes of others can be appropriate for institutional, as well as individual, self-reflection. Library user studies frequently reveal that patron perceptions of the library are at odds not only with our own opinions, but also with our goals for a particular service. The ERIAL project provided a unique opportunity for the Brookens Library to learn more about how students perceived the space in the library. As it turned out, the master planning process for the renovation of the building was working on a different timetable than the ERIAL Project, which unfortunately prevented the results from informing the design of the master plan. However, data from the ERIAL study has been, and will continue to be, compared to the assumptions that informed the master plan. The ERIAL study for the most part affirmed the conclusions of the master plan, and based on suggestions from both studies, interim changes are being made to Brookens Library spaces. Data from the ERIAL study will also be used to inform the final design plans for the future library renovation.

Of the five libraries participating in ERIAL, UIS was the only one to address the issue of space in a formal manner. We included this aspect for two reasons: to follow up on feedback from the LibQual+ survey of 2007 that suggested a difference in preference for quiet study space between older, commuter students and younger residential students; and to inform a high-level redesign plan for the Brookens Library facility, which was to begin in September 2008, just a month before the ERIAL Project began. UIS adapted several of the techniques that had been used to elicit perceptions and opinions about space by Foster and Gibbons at the University of Rochester (Foster and Gibbons 2007), including design workshops, photo diaries, and flip charts, in addition to using a cognitive mapping methodology and ethnographic interviews.

Although all five participating institutions in the ERIAL study used the same questions for the ethnographic interviews (see appendix A), UIS added one question to the ethnographic interviews that specifically addressed space. We explained to participants that we were in the midst of planning for a renovation of the building and asked, "If there was something that you could change about the building, what would it be?" Another question (included in all the interviews) concerned what students liked and disliked about the library. That question elicited nearly as many comments about space as the question that directly addressed the building, indicating that for many students the library is represented by the physical space—not its services, nor people, nor website. Because the interviews were open-ended in nature, we found that a substantial amount of information about the library building was gleaned from the student interviews, and many students provided rich descriptions of their perceptions of, and wishes about, library spaces.

COGNITIVE MAPPING

During the first year of the ERIAL Project, a cognitive mapping exercise was conducted with student participants in the campus cafeteria (dessert treats were offered as an incentive to volunteer for the exercise).[2] This methodology was carried out away from the library building to gain a larger student sample, hopefully including some students who may not have been regular library users, and also to learn what elements of the building students remembered without any visual clues. A total of twenty-three students participated in this activity on two different days during the spring semester, 2009.

To complete the cognitive mapping exercise, students were given a blank piece of paper along with blue, green, and red pens. They were then given six minutes to draw a map of the library from memory, and were asked to change the color of the pen every two minutes. This approach allowed the researchers to learn the order in which the map was drawn. Other than these two requirements, the students had wide latitude about how to interpret the instructions. Thus, the results varied significantly ranging from a three-dimensional approach to an all-floors approach, to an approach which focused only on the main entry level—the most common approach.

The drawings were analyzed by the research team to see which elements of the building and the library's services appeared most frequently. Almost all (91 percent) of the students identified Level 2, the main level of the library. Three elements were identified by 82 percent of the students:

the information/circulation desk, the computer stations, and the book stacks. Seventy-eight percent of students identified a front entrance to the building, and 73 percent drew the central stairway, an architecturally prominent feature of the building. After that, common elements quickly slipped below 50 percent, with only 17 percent of students identifying the librarians' offices and only a few seeming to be aware of the video/audio collections on the main floor. None of the students drew the government documents collection, which occupies a significant amount of floor space on Level 2.

Because of the nonrandom nature of our sample, we refrained from drawing universal conclusions from the cognitive maps on their own, but taken together with information from other methodologies, they helped us to come to some conclusions about students' understanding of the library's physical space and of its services, including the following.

Very few students could render the library's physical space with any degree of accuracy. Individual interviews with students suggested that this is related to the confusing layout of the library's floors. This also confirms observations by the architects of the Brookens Library master plan that the lack of any 90-degree angles in the building, while rendering the building architecturally interesting, makes way-finding much more difficult. In addition, the fact that the building is divided on the upper floors compounds this problem. One of the main goals of the master plan is to make the building more transparent and to make way-finding easier.

For most students, the entry level (Level 2) of the building is the building's focal point, as is evidenced by the high frequency of students drawing the floor itself and the individual features contained on it. Computer workstations and study areas were prominent in the students' mental image of the library, suggesting a high relative importance of these areas. Students also identified the information/circulation desks both frequently and accurately, suggesting that they do know conceptually where to seek help if they need it.

Much of the library's high-traffic floor space is devoted to elements that the students identified infrequently, such as new books, audio/music collection and seating area, and video shelves. The low number of students identifying the librarians' offices on the maps suggests that students have little contact with reference librarians or don't know where to find them. Individual interviews with students also supported this conclusion.

DESIGN WORKSHOPS

Two design workshops were conducted during spring semester of 2010, almost a year after the design charrettes were conducted by the master plan architects. The processes employed by the architects and the ERIAL Project anthropologist were remarkably similar. The nineteen students who participated in the ERIAL design workshops were asked to brainstorm about the tasks and activities they completed in the library and what they liked and disliked about the building. In addition, they were asked to describe their ideal library space and, finally, to sketch one floor of this ideal library space.

The design workshops were conducted in the library's café area (see figure 8.2) during a period when it was closed. Interestingly, the students talked a lot about how much they liked that space and then used it as the starting point for their ideal library space. Some students' drawings included a 24-hour computer lab, study areas, and the café.

One of the students drew in a "tutor table," which was noteworthy, since the master plan calls for the Center for Teaching and Learning (the group responsible for student tutoring) to move into the main service floor of the library. For this group, the library as a study space emerged

FIGURE 8.2 *The Brookens Library café area (viewed from above)*

as the priority. However, when asked if a computer lab on campus would serve the same purpose just as well, the students said that they wanted proximity and easy access to the library's collections, not just access to computers. In general, the design workshops confirmed directions taken by the architects in the master plan and conclusions that were beginning to form from information collected by other means.

FLIP CHARTS

Near the end of the ERIAL Project we borrowed one of the simplest tools that the University of Rochester had utilized in its study of library space (Foster and Gibbons 2007, 21): flip charts. These were deployed at strategic locations throughout the library, with two questions written at the top of a large piece of paper, "What do you like about this space?" and "What is missing from this space?" as well as a column for answers. We left the flip charts accessible for about a week, refreshing the sheets each day, as silliness tended to creep in after a while. Although the responses on the flip charts were, for the most part, not new, they did reinforce the data that we had obtained using other methods.

On the flip chart sheets, the instances of reporting a "quiet study area" as a positive desire increased as the floors got higher—even though both Levels 3 and 4 are designated as quiet study areas, students identified Level 4 as a quieter floor than Level 3. They also cited natural light as a reason that they like to come to Level 4 of the library. A guiding assumption in library design is to give people natural light and to protect books from the light, so it was surprising that the issue of the presence or absence of natural light did not come up in our other methods of soliciting information from students. The flip chart method, as quick and cheap as it is, proved to be the best method for giving us detailed information that we can act on in the short run. For instance, we have purchased new chairs because the students identified uncomfortable and dirty old furniture as a problem throughout the building. In the future, when we receive approval to pre-pare construction documents, we will want to go back to the students for more specific information about the placement of furniture and particular library functions and services.

Students answered the "what do you like about this space" question in terms of the building itself, as we expected. Interestingly, however, one-third to one-half of the negative flip chart comments related not to the building, but to services or collections. The most frequent response to the "what is missing from this level" question was "24/7 study area," followed by suggestions about updating the collection and getting rid of all those "horribly out-of-date" books. The desire for a 24/7 study area had also been expressed in the design workshops. Despite the statistics confirming low building usage late in the evening, the idea that the library should be open much longer hours persists, and it is one of the issues that the ERIAL Project is causing us to wrestle with once again.

ETHNOGRAPHIC INTERVIEWS AND PHOTO DIARIES

Ethnographic interviews were conducted with 35 students, a little less than half (42.9 percent) of whom were juniors. About a quarter (22.9 percent) of the participants were seniors, and an equal number (eight) were graduate students. Oddly enough, even though UIS is now admitting first-year students, all but nine of the interviewees were from the traditional "bread and butter" of UIS students—upper division and graduate students. Twenty-five of the interviewees (nearly 75 percent) were female, a figure that was reversed in the design workshops, where over 75 percent of participants were male. The interview participants reflected the racial mix at UIS (70 percent white; 20 percent black; with various other responses) and were spread across disciplines, with the highest number in social sciences, followed by humanities. As noted above, responses about the building were elicited not only from the particular question about library space, but also in reply to what the respondent liked or did not like about the building. Ten students participated in the photo diary methodology (see chapter 1), which included specific photographs and questions about the Brookens Library's space. The demographics of these participants were closely aligned with the interview respondents, and we will discuss these results along with the interview responses below.

To our surprise, the most nuanced comments about library space came not from any of the specific methodologies relating to space which we employed, but from the general interviews. These interviews tended to flesh out the information garnered from the other more space-specific methodologies. Notably, one of the major problems that the library redesign set out to address—that of way-finding—was confirmed by the students whom we interviewed. Many students said things such as, "It's like a maze up there"; "I get almost lost looking for a book because it's so confusing because of the circular design"; "It's very easy to get lost."

We had heard students say over the years that it would be nice to have librarians available on levels 3 and 4 of the library but we had never understood why until we read the transcripts from this study—not only were some students getting lost in the stacks because of the building design, but also they simply didn't know how to find books. One student suggested "thematic" signage for the book stacks instead of Library of Congress call number ranges (so the books in PS, for instance, would be labeled "American literature"), an idea we are considering more fully. We have also ordered badges for all public services workers (librarians, staff, and students) to wear so that students will be able to readily identify library employees and ask for help.

From reading the interview transcripts, one gets the impression that students either love or hate the building. For example, a 37-year-old female political science major, who is a junior, had this response to the question about likes and dislikes about the library: "I don't think there is anything I don't like about it . . . When I first hit this library, I was like, 'oh, they need to build an altar' . . . I was just in awe. It was like harps started playing or something." On the other hand, a 23-year-old male political science graduate student said, in response to the question about changing anything about the library space, "If I could do anything . . . personally I would just tear the whole building down."

Some students spoke at length about what they liked or did not like about the building. Many students liked the third and fourth levels for the quiet study areas that can be found there, and elaborated on what they found pleasing or not. One 20-year-old female, a junior in sociology/ anthropology, said, "There are a bunch of different nooks and crannies that you can go study in and it's quiet. It's just kind of cozy." Another student, 21, a female clinical lab science major, talked about how these spaces helped her to focus—"it's kind of like little corners that you can just sit in and be alone and focus on what you are trying to do." A 25-year-old male communications major said that the most important thing that he would tell a new freshman about the library would be that on the fourth floor "there are several computers [that] no one ever uses . . . you can be quiet. A peaceful area to do research or stuff like that." On the other hand, a 53-year-old female environmental studies graduate student observed that there is such a thing as it "being too quiet"—she would prefer a less isolated study area. Another student described the quiet areas favored by many of the students as being "creepily empty," and a few students raised concerns about personal security.

While the cognitive mapping exercises and the design workshops were dominated by Level 2, the main level, in the interviews and photo diaries the predominant theme was this push/pull between the desire for quiet study spaces and the need to work in groups, or simply to see and be seen. One 20-year-old female business major explained that she prefers Level 4 because it is quiet and a good place to collaborate in a group study. The main level is less desirable because friends see her and interrupt her work. Other students said that they liked the computers on Level 2 but found that some of them were too close together and there was not enough privacy. Occasionally, we would read a transcript where the student was able to articulate in more detail something that has been stated or hinted at by other students. This 31-year-old male political science graduate student was one of those. He appreciated the availability of computers on the upper levels of the building but he likes to have people around him when he studies, so for that reason he gravitated to Level 2; he felt disconnected from people on the fourth floor. On the other hand, he wished that Level 2 could be quieter like the upper levels. If he could change anything about the library, he would make it "more connected and open."

CONCLUSIONS

As we reviewed the data relating to library space, we realized that our hypothesis about preferences for quiet library space based on age or residential status had been too simplistic and was not supported. We found, surprisingly, that across all ages and living arrangements (commuting or on campus) the preference for quiet study spaces was nearly universal. However, many students also expressed the desire for more group study areas, including places with large tables where people could work together and spread their things out. We had posited an either/or situation, but found a much more nuanced approach to space on the part of students, depending on what types of work they wanted to accomplish.

Although implementing many of the solutions to issues raised by the ERIAL Project will have to wait for a comprehensive renovation, some solutions have already been put into place, and others are planned for the near future. For example, to respond to students' comments about the dirty and worn furnishings (a sentiment that was also highlighted in the master plan), task chairs (nearly 100) matching new models in the information commons were ordered for the rest of the library, and lounge chairs (13) were purchased to replace some of the most worn and outdated chairs. Unfortunately, financial constraints prevented us from replacing all of the old furniture. Lighting was also identified as a problem by both the student interview subjects and the master plan. Although the majority of lighting issues cannot be addressed now, we did order lamps for study tables in some of the gloomier sections of the building. The need for more and clearer signage repeatedly came up among our student interviewees. We will bring this need to the attention of Campus Building Services, the group responsible for all campus signage, and work with them to develop a solution. Finally, an issue that came up in terms of the building but which represents a service desire is the plea for longer library hours. The campus lacks a 24-hour computer lab, and we will work with Information Technology Services to see if there is some area on campus that could be designated for this purpose.

The ERIAL Project and the master plan study were in a way like competing polar expeditions: traversing the same landscape at slightly different times, they both ended up in the same place. The study has confirmed many directions of the master plan: the desire to bring in other services to the main level of the library, the need for better furnishings and lighting, and the vexing problem of noise. A renovation will greatly improve the acoustics of the building, but beyond that, we now understand that students want both to collaborate and to have quiet spaces. The student who wanted the library to be both more connected and more open hit upon a guiding principle of the design—this is what the renovated building hopes to achieve. In order to meet these, and future needs, we have resolved to continue consulting with our students, faculty, and other patrons as we finalize design plans and move forward with construction. In this way, we hope to ever more clearly see ourselves as others see us.

NOTES

1. For an explanation of the LibQual+ methodology, see http://www .libqual.org/home.

2. Much of this section is excerpted from the report by Andrew Asher, "University of Illinois at Springfield Library Cognitive Mapping Survey, Preliminary Report."

9

Transformative Changes in Thinking, Services, and Programs

LYNDA M. DUKE

The Ames Library is a beautiful five-story building and is considered the "intellectual heart" of Illinois Wesleyan University.[1] The library opened in January 2002 and employs approximately 70 student assistants during the academic year, 11 staff members, and 9 library faculty. Since its opening day, it has been clear, both from actual gate counts as well as anecdotal comments, that the library is much beloved on campus by students, faculty, staff, and visitors alike. The library faculty and staff take great pride not only in the beauty and comfort of the physical space, but also in the services provided to our users, and the quality and range of the print and online collection.

A substantial amount of thought went into designing and building the Ames Library—careful consideration that will serve the IWU community well for the foreseeable future. Nonetheless, over the last nine years, changes to services as well as the physical environment have been made within the library, in large part to reflect the information revolution occurring outside its walls. For example, the largest change involved the music library on the third floor, which historically had been housed separately on IWU's campus. In 2008 the music collection became integrated into the main stacks and the physical space became the Thorpe Center, a collaborative endeavor between Information Technology Services, the Mellon Center for Teaching & Learning, and the library. The Thorpe Center welcomes faculty, staff, and students and provides support and opportunities to become acquainted with new technologies. The services offered are designed to help integrate standard and emerging technologies within and outside the classroom. In addition, assistive technologies are housed at this location.

Certainly, over the last decade, there have been constant efforts by the library to respond to the perceived needs of the IWU community. What has been consistently missing in these attempts, however, was a solid understanding of how our students actually used the library. The ERIAL Project provided a depth and breadth of information about IWU students that allowed the library faculty to develop, for the first time, a nuanced and detailed understanding of IWU students and their interactions with librarians and library resources. This knowledge has transformed our thinking, thus helping us to make informed decisions about how to change or modify library services and programs. This chapter will focus on the process of identifying, selecting, and prioritizing these changes within the library and will describe the specific actions already taken, those in process, and plans for the future.

CHANGES IMPLEMENTED AS A RESULT OF THE ERIAL PROJECT

A series of changes to library services occurred while the ERIAL Project was under way, including a significant change to the library's reference service model in the fall of 2009. After considerable deliberation and many "lively" conversations, the library faculty determined that continuing to ask librarians to staff the information desk (formerly called the reference desk) was simply not an effective use of their time due to the low number of reference interactions. It is common knowledge in the library community that reference statistics have been declining throughout the academic world, and the Ames Library is no exception. According to the National Center for Education Statistics, as reported by the Academic Library Survey, reference statistics at academic libraries dropped 32 percent between 2000 and 2008 (Carey and Justh 2004, 26; Phan et al. 2009, 6). This continued the decline experienced in the early to mid-1990s (Martell 2008, 5). During this same period reference statistics at IWU also declined, although it is difficult to ascertain by exactly how much, as changes in how reference transactions were recorded make it impossible to accurately summarize transaction statistics.

IWU's new research assistance model consists of an on-call system that allows librarians to be accessible as needed. Student assistants now staff the information desk every hour the library is open. Librarians remain in their offices during their on-call time (rotated among all librarians). Both student assistants and librarians monitor the instant messaging service. Thus, library faculty are able to continue other work when not called upon to provide assistance to library users. Librarians post their office hours and on-call hours (outside their office and online). An added benefit is that students are already familiar with the concept of office hours with teaching faculty. Additionally, the decision was made to stop using the term *reference* and use *research assistance* in hopes that this would provide more clarity to the type of support a librarian can provide.

The Ames Library faculty had discussed changing the way we provided our reference services for a number of years prior to actually doing so. The decision was ultimately made when it became clear through the ERIAL data that the reason our reference numbers were low was due, in large part, to the fact that our students had no idea why they might reach out to a librarian. While the majority of students we interviewed struggled with one or more aspects of academic research, very few students actually reported seeking help from a librarian. In fact, one of the most striking aspects of the study was the near-invisibility of librarians within the academic worldview of IWU students. We learned that students went to librarians for help locating a physical item (a book in the stacks), but it did not seem to occur to them to go to librarians for searching or research-related questions, such as how to use a library database, how to find scholarly articles, or how to create a search strategy. For example, when asked if she had ever asked a librarian for help with a paper, a sophomore in international studies explained, "Not really actually. I've never done that. I always assume librarians are busy doing library stuff and it's just not the first thing that pops into my head when I think of a librarian, like helping with papers or paper writing." In fact, IWU students reported being very likely to ask other students for help—seeking out students that have either taken the class, are currently in the class, are majoring in the discipline, or have some other perceived expertise. Students also discussed reaching out to their professors, as they are seen as experts in the discipline, and they assign the course grades. One student replied quite bluntly when asked about seeking help from a librarian, "I don't want to sound crude, but I just don't feel like it's any of their business to. I don't know who any of them are. "

Moreover, some students noted during their interviews that they were not sure where to find a librarian—despite the fact that librarians were sitting at the information desk, which is in a highly visible location on the entry level. On the cognitive mapping exercise (see chapter 1 for a description of this methodology), only 11 percent of the students noted a librarian's office on the map—and of those rare students who actually drew a stick figure at the information desk, not one labeled it "librarian." Clearly, our presence at the information desk was not being noted by our students.

Without the ERIAL data to provide context for our declining reference statistics, it is not clear if, or when, the library faculty would have been able to break from tradition and implement a new way of providing this service. Once librarians were able to understand that *location* was not the main issue, it became an easier decision to restructure our work. Now the emphasis is placed on educating students and faculty about *why* students will benefit from the help of a librarian, along with information about where to find us. Although the revised model is still relatively new, it is encouraging to note there was an 18 percent increase in research questions from the academic year 2008–2009 to the academic year 2009–2010.

In conjunction with changing how we provide our research assistance, we also created a new logo: AskAmes (see figure 9.1). This was designed by a student assistant and is now prominently displayed on the library web pages, as well as used consistently in library marketing efforts. The AskAmes link describes not only the multiple ways to contact librarians (instant messaging, e-mail, phone, librarian's office hours, information desk), but also why a student might wish to do so. During this time period, the decision was

FIGURE 9.1
AskAmes Logo

also made to hire a student assistant to design all graphics for marketing pieces. Because the ERIAL data was revealing just how out of touch we were in understanding our students, we also realized that it would be beneficial to have a student involved in creating marketing pieces. This has brought a fresh, more colorful, and edgier look to our posters, flyers, and giveaways.

The results of the ERIAL study clearly supported our sense that students love the Ames Library as a physical space. As evidenced by the data from the mapping diary exercise (see chapter 1 for a description of this methodology), the majority of IWU students visit the library multiple times during any given day and use the space for a variety of purposes, including individual and group study, social interactions, and meetings for extracurricular activities. In addition to the steady stream of positive comments regarding the physical space, two consistent requests were a café and more group study rooms. During the spring of 2009, after years of discussion, the library faculty decided to consolidate the print journals—which were occupying a substantial part of the entry level—to make way for a café and more study space. Although these changes do not provide the group study rooms requested, this newly designed area is experiencing heavier use.

Prior to the ERIAL Project, the above changes had been discussed for varying lengths of time by library faculty, with no ability to reach consensus and implement changes. The detailed, qualitative data provided by the study guided our thinking and allowed us to move forward in a more streamlined and effective way to address these long-standing, and at times contentious, issues.

In addition, and perhaps more significantly, the data have allowed us to be more effective in forging stronger ties with teaching faculty, students, and administrators and to make substantial progress on integrating our work throughout the university. As the ERIAL Project findings became known across campus (through informal channels as well as a formal presentation to the IWU community) and teaching faculty and administrators began to grasp that our students lacked the appropriate information literacy skills, a number of new opportunities started to materialize and solidify. It must be noted that the groundwork laid by IWU librarians over the last decade or so was instrumental in helping to create these new accomplishments. Combining this foundational work with institution-specific, concrete data significantly increased our ability to assimilate our work into the overall fabric of the university.

For example, librarians are now given time during the annual summer Parent's Orientation Day (for parents of entering first-year students) to talk about the importance of information literacy skills and library resources. Working with the Admissions Office, librarians send a personalized welcome letter to all incoming students highlighting library resources and services—especially our personal research assistance. This fall, for the first time, librarians will be included in the Academic Expectations session required for all entering students during orientation. As this session is designed to highlight the most important aspects of the academic experience at IWU, we feel it is critical to be part of this presentation. Additionally, the library has been granted time during fall orientation to administer an information literacy test to all incoming students every three years. This will allow us to build a rich longitudinal data set to use in conjunction with the qualitative data we are collecting with our ongoing ethnographic research.

This past academic year grants were made available through the Writing Center, so that librarians and teaching faculty could work together to integrate information literacy into courses, including the redesign of assignments and the integration of librarians in the classroom. On a larger scale, exploratory discussions are under way with the associate dean of curriculum and the Curriculum Council regarding formal ways of integrating information literacy into the curriculum. The director of the writing program and the library are just beginning to consider innovative ways of integrating the Writing Center and the library. Finally, librarians are experiencing an increased demand for research instruction sessions and are having significant success embedding themselves in the required first-year writing course, required courses for various majors, and capstone courses.

IDENTIFYING, SELECTING, AND PRIORITIZING SERVICE CHANGES AS A RESULT OF THE ERIAL PROJECT

In addition to the changes implemented during the project and the new opportunities that developed as a result of the findings, a formalized process of generating new service change ideas began early in the project, while the ERIAL research team was still in the process of collecting data. As

the team began to observe students, discuss findings, and identify emerging patterns, we began to take notes of ideas, thoughts, concerns, possible
changes, and general areas to consider and investigate more thoroughly.
Ideas quickly began to multiply during the analysis phase of the project.
By spring of 2010, we had a list of sixty-five different items to consider.
These were captured in an Excel spreadsheet, along with a short description of the issue, the rationale for why it was important, and the potential
"fix." The items were roughly categorized into themes or areas, such as
"changes directed at librarians," "service changes directed at students,"
"website," and "space."

As we entered the final stages of our analysis, a corresponding step
involved members of the IWU team (with the exception of the resident
anthropologist) looking at each item and ranking it for the level of importance and feasibility on a scale of 1 to 3, with 3 being the most important
or feasible.[2] An average score for each item was generated and the team
then refined the items and rationale, eliminating duplication or issues
identified as not clear or specific enough, and restructuring the categories
slightly.

The next step was to share the document with all nine library faculty,
explain how the research team had created the list, and ask for input on
how to proceed. The librarians agreed that at this time the document
should be shared with all library staff, in order to encourage their engagement with the process. Although many of the identified items related to the
work of librarians, there were some issues that would impact the work of
staff as well. Moreover, given the importance of the findings and the scope
of the document, the librarians wanted the staff's general thoughts and
input. The document was shared with library staff a week before the sched-
uled librarian/staff meeting in the hopes of providing staff enough time to
reflect on the document. During the meeting, the lead research librarian
provided a brief overview of the project and details on how the list was
created. Unfortunately, but not surprisingly, there were few comments or
questions and very little conversation took place. Given that this is a typical response in many staff meetings, although disappointing, this lack of
engagement was not seen as a reflection of the contents of the document.

All librarians were then asked to rank each item for level of importance, again on a scale of 1 to 3, with 3 being the most important. The
library faculty submitted their rankings to the lead research librarian, who

generated an average score for each item. There was remarkable consistency regarding scores. This phase of the process resulted in the ranking of five items as a perfect "3": continue strengthening relationships with teaching faculty; provide consistent information throughout the library; provide consistent training at service points; create a core common skills set for all service points staffed by student assistants; and actively encourage teaching faculty to have library liaison and discipline-specific research guide information on all syllabi (details of these items are discussed in the following section).

The research team further refined the items, with some placed in the categories of "already in process," or "to drop." At this juncture, the items ranked as generally "undoable" or low priority were added to the "to drop" section. For example, one item suggested that we "create a culture of seeking help." This emanated from our observations that students do not appear to ask for help when they hit obstacles while conducting searches for information. We often observed students changing databases, topics, and/or giving up on locating a source, but not seeking help, as illustrated by the statement made by a senior in women's studies: "If I don't have access to it [a source], I search for something else." While creating a culture of seeking help was rated a high priority and is certainly a laudable goal, the library faculty were unable to generate any specific and reasonable ways to accomplish this goal. Likewise, some students requested quiet zones in the library, while others requested group study zones. Enforcing these requests seemed undoable and both were dropped from the list.

This process narrowed the list to thirty items. It was particularly gratifying to the IWU research team that there was tremendous agreement in both the list of items considered to be of highest priority and those that should be dropped. Moreover, all librarians felt that we had identified issues to pursue of a substantive nature, with high potential to positively impact our users. Although some aspects were believed to be major undertakings, they were also deemed achievable—albeit with concentrated efforts and resources.

The final stage of this process took place at the annual retreat for library faculty, in early August 2010, not quite two years after beginning the project. The identified issues were further broken down into specific action items to be completed. Specific responsibilities for accomplishing the identified tasks were assigned to individuals in the library. In most cases, tasks were easily assigned by functional areas: for example, information literacy issues were to be coordinated by the information literacy librarian, marketing issues by the academic outreach librarian, and so forth. This was both a crucial and exciting phase of the process. Often data is collected, but the will, or time, to create concrete steps and implement changes is missing. However, by moving so seamlessly into this stage, it was apparent that the findings from the ERIAL Project would help to propel the library forward.

FIVE AREAS OF CHANGE

The most important areas identified to work on as a result of the ERIAL Project were broken into the following five categories:

1. Relationships with teaching faculty and university administrators
2. Library web pages/website-related
3. Marketing and assessment
4. Information literacy
5. Student assistant training

The following section provides a description of each of these categories, as well as specific goals to pursue and accompanying rationale.

CATEGORY ONE
Continue to Develop and Strengthen Relationships with Teaching Faculty and University Administrators, Explaining Library Services and Resources

The data from the ERIAL Project suggested that teaching faculty play a critical role in socializing students to the expectations and demands of college-level academic research. Thus, faculty members are crucial to facilitating relationships between students and librarians. In short, students follow the lead and recommendations of their instructors when seeking out and interacting with librarians and library resources. Therefore, educating faculty about library services and resources educates students by extension, while building relationships between faculty members and librarians simultaneously builds relationships with students. Although developing relationships directly with students must be continued through a variety of avenues, focusing additional library outreach activities on developing faculty relationships may prove to be more effective, given the role faculty play in students' lives. Moreover, faculty leave and enter the university at a much slower rate than students and there are fewer faculty to work with than students.

Because teaching faculty are ultimately responsible for grading an assignment, information gleaned from professors is highly valued by students, while librarians are not always viewed as possessing the disciplinary expertise to provide sufficient assistance. IWU students view professors as experts in their fields of study, and when the professor specifically recommends working with a librarian the students tend to highly value this advice. Professors therefore regularly act as gatekeepers who mediate when and how students get in touch with librarians as they are working on research assignments. In this way, the attitude of professors toward librarians is a key determining factor in developing student/librarian relationships.

As teaching faculty become more knowledgeable about library resources and services, as well as the importance of teaching information literacy skills, the hope is that they will adjust assignments accordingly, refer students to librarians, and be more likely to request research instruction sessions in their courses. The ERIAL study has provided a wealth of evidence that can be used to illustrate the importance of including library instruction sessions in courses. As a first-year student noted, "I would not have gotten an A in Gateway if it had not been for that lab [library instruction] session."[3]

Because IWU employs the library liaison model (where each librarian is assigned to work with one or more academic departments on campus to develop the collection, work one-on-one with students, and provide in-class instruction sessions), the work of this category was deemed the responsibility of all library faculty. Five core goals were established for this category:

1. Library faculty will encourage all teaching faculty in their liaison areas to include information about the related online research guide and the librarian's contact information and office hours on syllabi and course pages (e.g., Moodle). Because students must

refer to the class syllabus throughout the semester, including this information may help to increase the librarian's visibility and legitimacy in the eyes of the students.

2. Librarians will regularly strategize and communicate with each other about their liaison roles and relationships. Each librarian has issues unique to their departments, yet each librarian has had success and challenges in working with teaching faculty—what can we learn from each other? This is now a standing agenda item at all librarian meetings. In addition, librarians share more of this information via e-mail and informal discussions, and an internal Libguide has been created to gather relevant readings, in-class exercises, handouts, and teaching strategies.

3. Library liaisons will encourage teaching faculty to review and offer suggestions for the discipline-specific research guides (in 2009 librarians began using Libguides). This may help to ensure appropriate resources are listed; perhaps spark discussions on how to revise or develop assignments; and professors may be more likely to suggest specific library resources to students because they are more familiar with available sources and have invested in the development of the research guide.

4. Librarians will encourage teaching faculty to introduce librarians and the online research guides to all classes during the first part of the semester. This may help to increase visibility and legitimacy, as well as to increase students' understanding of how a librarian can help and the available library resources and services.

5. To the extent possible, library faculty will seek out ways to work with teaching faculty on developing assignments, incorporating the use of library resources and ways to integrate teaching information literacy skills in courses.

CATEGORY TWO
Changes to the Library Web Pages/Website-Related

In many ways the library's web pages have become the face of the library and the backbone of the library's work, playing a central role unimaginable two decades ago. All users, as well as library faculty and staff, rely on the website to provide up-to-date, accurate, and easy-to-access information, as well as sophisticated and comprehensive databases with access to academic and scholarly sources. Incorrect or outdated information, fragmented entry points, and antiquated databases (relative to the ease of search engines on the Internet) all create barriers to our users.

The ERIAL Project demonstrated that when students encountered obstacles, either in the form of fragmented tools of scholarship (a myriad of library databases) or technical issues (such as dead links, slow response time, or incomplete information in an ILLiad request form), this often resulted in the student abandoning the source in question and beginning a search for different items or reverting to Google. In general, IWU students are very quick to give up on finding a source, so much so that almost any obstacle they encounter will cause them to move on to another source or to change their research topic.

Therefore, library faculty are in agreement that every attempt should be made to provide tips and training for navigating the library website and streamlining services and resources where possible. The Library Web Team was assigned the responsibility of working toward seven core goals:

1. Create a site map to provide an additional navigational tool for individuals looking for specific information on our web pages.

2. Provide up-to-date, succinct, and comprehensive point-of-use explanations of library tools. Currently, users may click on certain links and find themselves on a web page with no explanation about the service or resource they need to use to access a resource. Users should be able to quickly ascertain what the service is, how to use it, and how to get more help if needed.

3. Add maps of the library stacks to the online catalog and update maps of the library on the website and within the library. Currently our students exhibit a great deal of difficulty locating items in the collection. Better navigational tools could prove useful when they are looking for a physical item.

4. Because we observed students treating all search boxes as a Google-like interface, the decision was made to conduct a trial of the EBSCO Discovery Service (EDS) from October 2010 to May 2011. Our current structure (where databases must be searched independently) clearly creates obstacles to using, finding, and

accessing academic resources. After observing students using EDS and our more traditional databases, the decision to subscribe to this new tool was made in the summer of 2011.

5. As a corollary to item four, the library should seek out creative ways to streamline library interfaces and services.

6. Create an online FAQ section. Creating a centralized list of FAQs could help users and student assistants better understand what resources are available, how to access and use them, and where to seek help if needed.

7. Provide information about library faculty on the banner portion of the library web page (a photo and areas of expertise). A key finding from the ERIAL study is that students are either confused about, or lack an understanding of, what librarians do and who librarians are.

CATEGORY THREE
Marketing and Assessment

There exists an ongoing need to inform our new and current students and teaching faculty about our services and resources, for four main reasons:

1. Our users enter IWU with varying degrees of comfort, experience, and exposure to library resources and services.

2. The library and information environment is constantly changing (both tools and available resources).

3. Although there may be overlap with other libraries with which students are familiar, the Ames Library is also unique in its offerings (particularly compared to high school libraries).

4. And finally, students find the Internet to be easy and effective to use and therefore may not see the need to use our resources. As one first-year student in math noted, "I'm lazy and I use the Internet."

Assessment and marketing are uniquely interlinked. To enhance our ability to effectively educate our users we need to fully understand how they use our services and resources and the obstacles they encounter while doing so, how students view the library, and what they think they need in order to conduct their research. In addition to providing insight on how best to market our services and resources, this information will also prove helpful in crafting our services and selection of resources. The academic outreach librarian was assigned the following four core goals for this category:

1. Create a series of videos, posters, and other related marketing items using students to tell other students what they should know about the library and its services and resources, and/or how they have benefited from using our resources and services. Our research shows that students talk to one another and seek each other out for advice. This should be leveraged to our benefit.
2. Continuously encourage students and faculty to go beyond the databases they usually use by marketing discipline-specific resources that are new, underutilized, or particularly important to a major, minor, or program. Participants in the study often reverted back to the same database they had success with before, whether or not it might be an appropriate source for their current project (see chapter 5 for related details).
3. Develop an ongoing, sustainable plan for using ethnographic methodologies to understand our users' needs, difficulties, and ways of conducting research, building on the substantial data gathered in the ERIAL Project.[4]
4. Because students do not tend to seek out librarians or our resources, we must make it as easy as possible for our users to learn about what the library has to offer and we should provide up-to-date information. This can be accomplished by reaching out to students and faculty using as many venues as possible: courseware, e-mail, electronic postings, one-on-one interactions, and a library blog.

CATEGORY FOUR
Information Literacy

From the ERIAL Project, we learned that many IWU students, to a surprising extent, are lacking information literacy skills, as defined by the Association of College and Research Libraries. In particular, students struggle with reading citations and identifying the type of source referenced, understanding why it is important to cite information and the information a citation conveys, or knowing when a citation is required. Many of our students do not fully understand issues surrounding the ethical use of information, especially with respect to the meaning and implications of copyright protection, and the practical actions required to correctly observe copyright law.[5]

IWU students exhibited difficulty in evaluating sources of information, and were particularly confused about the differences between primary and secondary sources. Finally, our research showed that students do not adequately understand how information resources are organized, both in the library and elsewhere (e.g., on the Internet). For example, students display difficulties understanding the difference between the library's catalog and online databases, the types of resources that can be found using these tools, and the differences between library subject-specific databases. As a first-year accounting student noted, "I don't really know what there is to use. I know there are books but I don't really know how to find them. Really the only thing I know how to do is go to Google and type in what I'm looking for."

Four core goals were generated for this area. These were woven into the library's information literacy document and fall under the purview of our information literacy librarian.

1. Seek ways to better integrate information literacy skills instruction throughout the curriculum and throughout a student's four years at IWU—from the required writing class for all first-year students through senior seminars. Doing so will help to build relationships between students and librarians over time, build skill sets as students gain disciplinary knowledge, and keep students (and teaching faculty) up-to-date with changing library services and resources.
2. Develop innovative ways to teach students elements of the research process, information literacy skills, and searching techniques.
3. Provide more and better information literacy tutorials on the library's website. Although not all students will take advantage of this type of instruction, providing yet another avenue for our users to learn information literacy skills may prove useful to some of our students.

4. Establish stronger ties with the university's Writing Center, in the hopes of providing another way for students to get referrals to librarians and/or help directly from other students regarding finding appropriate sources for their assignments.

Student Assistant Training

The Ames Library employs approximately 70 students during the academic year and 15–18 during the summer months. Library faculty and staff rely on student assistants to staff all four service points (Tate Archives, Thorpe Center, information desk and circulation desk). Often, when a user seeks assistance the first person (and sometimes the only person) they encounter is a student. The ERIAL Project provided compelling data that demonstrates the importance of having well-trained students who can provide consistent and appropriate service. Our research shows that our students often had difficulty locating books or other items in the library stacks. Unfortunately, when students sought help for locating these items at one of the service points, many times they were given incomplete or incorrect information by student assistants.

Three core goals were established for this category, which were incorporated into the work of the training team (consisting of library faculty and staff who supervise student assistants).

1. Create a set of core common skills for all student assistants who work in the library. Although not all students work at service desks, all student assistants should have a basic understanding of the library and our services and resources. Examples of common skills include how to read a call number, locate contact and office hour information for librarians, and find designated information using the library web page.
2. Develop a system to track inquiries (quantity and type) at all four service points. This will help us to better understand the types of questions we are receiving at the different locations and modify how student training is developed.
3. Provide consistent information and training (using consistent terminology) at all four service points. Our students do not tend

to ask for help very often; when they (and other users) do so, we want to provide excellent service. Because library jargon is confusing to students and faculty, and even more when used inconsistently, librarians should minimize the use of jargon, online, in print, and in conversation, and consistent terminology should be used for services and resources.

CONCLUSION

As noted in the introduction to this chapter, the ERIAL Project provided a level of detail about IWU students that was previously unavailable. In the process of closely observing our students over the course of eighteen months, some of our initial assumptions were confirmed, such as their love for the library as a physical space—as one student noted, "It's the way a library should look." We also suspected that our students procrastinate, and this trait was mentioned repeatedly when interviewing students. It is worth noting that this did not diminish their expectations for immediate access to the needed source, as stated by a first-year math student, "Yeah I procrastinate, but when I want something, I want it now."

Of greater importance, however, was the bright light shed on issues not previously understood, such as how quickly students gave up when encountering a perceived obstacle or how little students understand the beneficial role a librarian can play in their research needs. Whereas we often did not like what we discovered, the library faculty at IWU are in a stronger position as a result of participating in this study.

This study allowed us to build a holistic understanding of our students and their rhythms and activities throughout the course of a typical day, and how they use (or do not use) the library spaces, services, and resources. We now have much needed qualitative and quantitative data to guide and support our decisions and actions. As a result, library faculty at IWU have been able to move forward with long-simmering, much-discussed and debated issues, as well as forge new goals to pursue and pathways for accomplishing our objectives.

In many ways, the end results of the ERIAL Project have yet to be determined, in that much of the follow-up work identified as a result of the study remains to be completed. However, progress is already being made on a variety of fronts. With an increased understanding of user needs, IWU librarians have begun to develop more effective models of service, tools of scholarship, relationships with teaching faculty and university administrators, and instructional techniques. As a direct result of the ERIAL Project, as well as sustained efforts by all the librarians at IWU, library faculty are now actively engaged in conversations with the associate dean of curriculum, writing coordinator for general education, the writing program director, and the interim provost to create avenues for interweaving information literacy into the curriculum.

It is clear that the study provided the context and details necessary to create a focused set of goals to work on for the foreseeable future. One might argue that many of the goals we have set for ourselves are not revolutionary. However, what is clear is that because we now have data instead of assumptions, the library faculty at IWU can proceed with confidence, clarity of purpose, and unity as we seek to understand the needs of our users, teach information literacy, and assess our success.

NOTES

1. Illinois Wesleyan University is a highly selective, private, liberal arts school with 2,100 undergraduate students.

2. The resident anthropologist helped guide the evaluation process. Since he was not a permanent member of the Ames Library faculty, he chose to refrain from ranking the items.

3. IWU requires all students to enroll in a writing course during their first year on campus. This "Gateway" course is a small, discussion-oriented class designed to develop students' critical thinking and writing skills.

4. Planning is under way to annually conduct research process and retrospective interviews with students, along with an information literacy test.

5. In the fall of 2009, the IWU research team implemented an information literacy pre- and post-test to over 50 percent of the entering class. The extensive qualitative data collected through the ERIAL Project provided a unique opportunity to contextualize the quantitative results from the information literacy tests.

10
Conclusions and
Future Research

ANDREW D. ASHER AND LYNDA M. DUKE

At the beginning of the ERIAL Project, none of the individuals involved with the study could have foreseen the specific paths traveled, lessons learned, conclusions drawn, or steps taken as a result of the research. Each of the five participating institutions set out to increase its knowledge about its own students and their research processes, as well as how relationships between students, teaching faculty, and librarians shape these processes. Although all of the research teams implemented many of the same methodologies and followed the same overall plan, each team eventually forged its own path, focusing in on particular aspects of the study that were most meaningful to their campus and university culture.

The ERIAL Project is distinctive in that the study provided site-specific data, as well as the ability to make cross-institution comparisons with select components of the data. For example, a recurring theme throughout the ERIAL Project, and across the five institutions, was the centrality of relationships between teaching faculty and librarians within students' research processes and practices. At the completion of this study, it seems fair to state that establishing strong relationships between librarians and faculty is critical to librarians' success in reaching students. Additionally, all institutions found students' search habits and information literacy skills to be lacking. The impact of the Internet on this generation of students is unequivocal—students expect instantaneous, online access to sources and they often lack the ability to refine searches and evaluate sources, in large part due to their years of successfully searching the Web for their information needs. Moreover, and perhaps most disconcerting, was the almost uniform lack of understanding regarding the work of a librarian and the specific ways in which they can support students in their research. Although heartening to know that those students who found their way to working with a librarian were satisfied with this experience, the abysmally low numbers of librarian-student interactions makes this, in the end, of scant comfort.

In addition to the common themes identified throughout the findings at the five ERIAL libraries, the ERIAL Project presented research teams with the rare opportunity to learn about specific needs and habits of their own students. By utilizing numerous methodologies, each site was able to create a more nuanced understanding of the daily lives of their students. This level of detail about one's own institution is critical if librarians are to effectively engage with their students. For example, some of the obstacles students face at a private, four-year, residential college (e.g., balancing the demands of coursework with athletics and extracurricular activities) are different than those found at an urban, Hispanic-Serving Institution (e.g., long commutes on public transportation, or juggling full-time jobs and course schedules). The chance to examine one's students in such close detail proved to be of extraordinary value for each university. In the daily working world of a library, it is common to make assumptions about different aspects of one's environment, in part because it is human nature to do so, but often because there are insufficient data available. Yet actions must be taken and decisions made. Clearly, the more distinctive and finely grained information we have about our students and their research habits, the more informed our choices and actions can be.

All of the chapters in this volume underscore the importance of understanding the library not just as a place or space, but as a social system comprised of a multitude of interactions between students, librarians, faculty members, staff, and administrators. As Thill notes in chapter 2, assumptions and attitudes contained within these relationships can have profound effects on the goals and expected outcomes of expectations for students' research. If they are unaware of differing expectations, librarians and faculty members can find themselves working at cross-purposes to the detriment not only of students, but also their continued and effective collaboration.

Tensions and miscommunications between faculty members and librarians can have a direct effect on the quality of library instruction, as well as whether or not a librarian is invited to give instruction at all. In chapter 3, Armstrong describes in detail the delicate balance between instructors and librarians in teaching research skills, as well as the importance of tailoring library services to meet the specific needs of individual courses and faculty members. The ERIAL Project teams repeatedly observed that teaching faculty's attitudes toward, and relationships with, librarians were key variables in determining when, and if, a student utilized a librarian for assistance with a research assignment.

Unfortunately, the invisibility of librarians within the academic lives of students was also a recurring theme throughout the ERIAL Project, as discussed by Miller and Murillo in chapter 4 and Asher and Duke in chapter 5. While probably not surprising to reference librarians, both chapters suggest that a central cause underlying this lack of use is that students do not have sufficient opportunity to build relationships with librarians, instead relying on the advice of their professors and peers.

Because of its diverse sample of students and universities, the results of the ERIAL Project helped elucidate issues that are institution-specific as well as those that are more generalizable. For example, across the ERIAL institutions, we observed students struggling with the concepts and mechanics of the search process, as well as the information literacy skills needed to appropriately evaluate source materials (see chapters 5–7). However, the ERIAL Project also demonstrated the importance of examining the specificity of individual universities and student groups, as well as developing intensive local knowledge of the unique social processes taking place in a single library. Ethnography is particularly well-suited to this task, as David Green demonstrates in his examination of Hispanic students at NEIU in chapter 6 and Firouzeh Logan and Elizabeth Pickard show in their study of first-generation college students at UIC in chapter 7. Both of these chapters illustrate the importance of understanding students' social context and backgrounds in developing effective library services.

In chapter 8, Jane Treadwell, Amanda Binder and Natalie Tagge demonstrate the process of utilizing ethnography to inform library planning by illustrating how ERIAL Project data was used to enhance the redesign of UIS library spaces. Likewise, Lynda Duke provides an in-depth discussion of how IWU integrated its ERIAL Project results directly into the process of planning and implementing service changes in chapter 9.

CONDUCTING ETHNOGRAPHY STUDIES IN LIBRARIES

While the ERIAL Project was fortunate to have funding for full-time anthropologists, a large grant is not necessary to begin applying ethnographic methods within any particular library setting. In general, ethnography is time-intensive, but not especially expensive, and very little specialized equipment is needed. In fact, the vast majority of the ERIAL Project funds went to paying staff salaries, and only a small percentage was spent on supplies and equipment (for details on timing and equipment, see Asher and Miller 2010). It is also important to note that although there are numerous methodologies that could be administered, it is also feasible, and perhaps even recommended, to start a project of this nature on a smaller scale, choosing a few methodologies particularly well-suited to one's community.

As an outcome of the ERIAL Project, Andrew Asher and Susan Miller (2010) developed a "toolkit" for librarians to use in planning and executing a 20–30-participant ethnographic study over the course of an academic year. An ethnographic study even of this size requires a significant time commitment. A one-hour interview typically requires at least three to four hours of analysis in addition to the time required to schedule, conduct, and transcribe the interviews. Successfully managing a project's overall workflow can also be a time-intensive endeavor. Nevertheless, time to think deeply about the data collected is a critical component of a successful ethnographic project, and any study should realistically gauge the amount of data that can be effectively collected and analyzed in the time available.

Additionally, ensuring that there is support from library personnel and the administration is crucial, for two main reasons. First, taking on a project of this nature will require those involved to put aside at least some of their usual responsibilities; others may be asked to take on added responsibilities to cover the library's normal work flow, and deadlines may need to be extended for some regular tasks to be accomplished. Second, in order to ensure that the findings generated can then be translated into action items, there needs to be "buy-in" from those who are not necessarily involved in the day-to-day work of the project. Frequent updates regarding the progress of the study and emerging themes from the data analysis can be helpful in fostering this investment.

While they might first appear daunting, ethnographic methods can be one of the most effective ways of learning about how practices occur in context, and are especially useful for understanding complex processes that are difficult to examine using surveys or other more quantitative approaches. Ethnography is a nuanced task of close observation, interrogation, and analysis, and is a skill that is best learned by building experience with practice. An ethnographic study of this kind requires careful planning, teamwork, administrative support, learning new skills, diligence, and an investment of time. As we hope the ERIAL Project has shown, however, the depth and breadth of information that ethnography provides are well worth the commitment required, and this is often one of the best ways to obtain holistic and actionable information about the needs and requirements of a library's various user groups.

At this juncture, it is also worth noting an unanticipated, yet highly valued, outcome of the project. Most of the research team members from the five institutions did not know each other prior to the study. Despite the geographic distance, many strong relationships evolved between the librarians involved in the project. These new ties will almost certainly help to forge new collaborative research, presentations, and general support of each others' work. Moreover, all research team members have benefited from developing a deeper understanding of the differences, and commonalities, among academic institutions in the state of Illinois.

FUTURE RESEARCH

Although there is now a growing body of literature illustrating the use of ethnographic methods in academic libraries (see chapter 1), there remains a great deal of space for future research. One important area demonstrated throughout the ERIAL Project is a need for increased study of high school and community college students, and in particular how the previous research experiences of these students affect their transition to four-year universities. At the ERIAL institutions with high numbers of transfer students, our results suggested a need for better outreach with the community colleges that send students to four-year universities (often this involves only a handful of sending institutions for a given four-year university). However, pursuing this question fell outside of the ERIAL Project's mandate.

At the other end of the spectrum, there is also a need for additional research directed at the more advanced information requirements of graduate students. While the ERIAL Project included some graduate student participants, the main focus of the study was on undergraduate research habits, and more data is necessary to determine the practices and unmet needs of graduate students as they make the transition to professional scholarship. The ERIAL Project also included online and distance education students at only one university (UIS), gathering sufficient preliminary information to suggest that these students' instructional needs and library use practices are distinct enough from on-campus students to warrant an additional study designed specifically for the online educational experience. Both of these avenues of research will only grow in importance as graduate students become a cohort with no pre-Internet memory and the overall number of courses taught online continues to increase.

Finally, library ethnography in general is in need of more substantive longitudinal data examining how students' research practices and information literacy skills change and develop over the course of a university curriculum. As a continuation of the ERIAL Project, IWU is in the process of designing and implementing an ongoing research strategy to address these longitudinal questions. In order to create a sustainable approach for collecting and analyzing data, a combination of quantitative data (in the form of an information literacy test) and qualitative data will be pursued. As noted in chapter 9, the findings from the ERIAL Project are driving numerous endeavors, either newly created or reenergized, within the Ames Library. The attention the ERIAL Project results have garnered on IWU's campus makes it even more compelling for librarians to put their energy into this type of work.

SUMMARY

It is clear that for many students, the term *librarian* and its related functions are antiquated and that the library is often viewed as a place to meet other students, study, or print needed documents, rather than being an integral part of their research and a place offering highly valued research assistance and resources. Growing up with the Internet has, for many of our students, meant never having to talk to a librarian. If the library community hopes to have students engage with the library and related services, we need to aggressively educate ourselves about their needs and habits, and then inform students and faculty about how our services and resources can benefit their immediate and long-term educational goals. If librarians wish to remain relevant in today's world, the profession must continue to actively seek ways to engage more deeply in the academic community. Sitting passively at the reference desk, waiting for students and faculty to find us, is no longer a sustainable model.

Through participating in the ERIAL Project, each institution discovered unique aspects about its students and the culture of its university, as well as some generalizable truths about this generation of learners. Based on its history, traditions, resources, politics, and philosophies, how a library uses this information to move forward toward achieving its vision will, in the end, be tailored specifically to that library's particular world.

ERIAL Interview Guide Questions

The following questions comprised the common interview guide that was shared across the five ERIAL universities. These questions were not intended to be an interview script, but rather to provide direction and structure to the interview. The researcher conducting the interview was therefore allowed to ask additional questions to follow up on interesting themes or topics and to clarify answers or elicit additional information. Institutional research teams were also allowed to add questions designed to address specific research questions that were of particular interest to their universities.

PREVIOUS PREPARATION

Did you write a long research paper or work on a large project before attending college?

If no:

- When did you—or when do you expect to—write your first paper or project in college?
- What do you think you will use as your primary sources of information?

If yes, or if the student mentions writing a college-level paper:

- What did you use as your primary sources of information?

EVALUATING RESEARCH PROJECTS

What would you describe as the elements of a good research project?

What do you think your professors are looking for when they grade your research projects?

RESEARCH PROCESS

Please describe the process you followed for the last research paper or project you worked on, step by step, from beginning to end. What did you do first, second, etc.?

If student is describing a current paper: Can you show me how you might look for information for this project here in the library?

How did you search for information sources for this project?

Where did you expect to find books and articles?

What about other types of information? For example, statistics, raw data sources, survey results, etc.?

What sources did you use for this project?

Can you demonstrate for me how you searched for these sources? (Ask the student to walk you through a search using the computer provided.)

What problems or obstacles did you encounter while working on this assignment? (Probe for specifics, e.g., finding good books and articles, time management issues, difficulty in judging appropriate source materials, etc.)

If you had to do this project again, what would you have done differently?

What help do you think the library could have offered you?

How do you think your research process compares to that of other students?

STUDENT-FACULTY EXPECTATIONS
AND INTERACTIONS

While you were working on your last research paper, when were the most important components of the project communicated to you by your instructor?

How do you apply the guidelines given to you for your research assignment to your work in the library?

SEEKING HELP

When was the last time you asked someone to help you with your research?

During the assignment you described earlier, did you find you needed help with any aspect of the project?

What kind of help did you need?

Who did you ask for help?

What kind of help did you expect to receive?

LIBRARIAN-STUDENT EXPECTATIONS
AND INTERACTIONS

Tell me about the last librarian you worked with on a research paper or project.

Were you surprised by the level of knowledge they expected of you?

What kind of help did you need from the librarian?

What other help did you need?

If answer is anything except "nothing": Did you get this help?

In general, how do you expect librarians to help students?

What is the most significant thing librarians can do to help students with their assignments?

When you work with a librarian, how would you most likely do this (e.g., instant messaging, phone, e-mail, librarian's office, reference desk, something else)?

(Optional) What do you expect of librarians during your research process?

(Optional) What are some of the most important resources or services that the library offers to students?

What do you expect librarians to know about technology? (Probe for explanation)

What do you think librarians expect of students?

What do you think librarians expect of students doing research?

DESIRED CHANGES AND IMPROVEMENTS

What do you like most about the university's library?

What don't you like about it?

Have you used the library website?

What do you like about it?

What don't you like about it?

If you could change one or two things about our library, what would they be?

Would you like to know more about the library and its services? If yes, what?

What do you wish librarians would tell students about the library?

Do you have a favorite place to study in the library? Why?

If you could tell an incoming freshman the most important thing he/she needs to know about the library, what would it be?

BIBLIOGRAPHY

Adkins, Denice, and Lisa Hussey. 2006. "The Library in the Lives of Latino College Students." *Library Quarterly* 76, no. 4: 456–80.

Alejo, Berenice. 2008. "The Latino Landscape: A Metro Chicago Guide and Non-Profit Directory." Institute for Latino Studies, University of Notre Dame. http://latinostudies.nd.edu/pubs/pubs/Latino_Landscape_Final2.pdf.

American Association of State Colleges and Universities. 2007. *Hispanic Student Success in State Colleges and Universities: Creating Supportive Spaces on Our Campuses*. New York: Author.

Antell, Karen, and Debra Engel. 2006. "Conduciveness to Scholarship: The Essence of Academic Library as Place." *College & Research Libraries* 67, no. 6: 536–60.

Applegate, Rachel. 2009. "The Library Is for Studying: Student Preferences for Study Space." *Journal of Academic Librarianship* 35, no. 4: 341–46.

Asher, Andrew, Lynda Duke, and Dave Green. 2010. "The ERIAL Project: Ethnographic Research in Illinois Academic Libraries." *Academic Commons* (May). http://www.academiccommons.org/commons/essay/erial-project.

Asher, Andrew, and Susan Miller. 2010. "So You Want to Do Anthropology in Your Library? or A Practical Guide to Ethnographic Research in Academic Libraries." http://www.erialproject.org/publications/toolkit/.

Association of College and Research Libraries (ACRL). 2010. "ACRL Objectives for Information Literacy Instruction: A Model Statement for Academic Librarians." http://www.ala.org/ala/mgrps/divs/acrl/standards/objectivesinformation.cfm.

———. 2000. "Information Literacy Competency Standards for Higher Education." http://www.ala.org/ala/mgrps/divs/acrl/standards/standards.pdf.

Beard, Jill, and Penny Dale. 2008. "Redesigning Services for the Net-Gen and Beyond: A Holistic Review of Pedagogy, Resource, and Learning Space." *New Review of Academic Librarianship* 14, no. 1: 99–114.

Beaver, William. 2010. "Do We Need More College Graduates?" *Society* 47, no. 4: 308–11.

Bennett, Scott. 2009. "Libraries and Learning: A History of Paradigm Change." *Portal: Libraries and the Academy* 9, no. 2: 181–97.

———. 2008. Editorial: "The Information or the Learning Commons: Which Will We Have?" *Journal of Academic Librarianship* 34, no. 3: 183–85.

———. 2007a. "Designing for Uncertainty: Three Approaches." *Journal of Academic Librarianship* 33, no. 2: 165–79.

———. 2007b. "First Questions for Designing Higher Education Learning Spaces." *Journal of Academic Librarianship* 33, no. 1: 14–26.

Blum, S. D. 2009. *My Word! Plagiarism and College Culture.* Ithaca, NY: Cornell University Press.

Bok, Derek. 2010. "College and the Well-Lived Life." *Chronicle of Higher Education* 56, no. 21: A36–37.

Branin, Joseph. 2010. Editorial: "Space, the Final Frontier." *College & Research Libraries* 71, no. 2: 96.

———. 2007. "Shaping our Space: Envisioning the New Research Library." *Journal of Library Administration* 46, no. 2: 27–53.

Brindley, Dame Lynne J. 2009. "Challenges for Great Libraries in the Age of the Digital Native." *Information Services & Use* 29, no. 1: 3–12.

Brophy, Peter. 2008. "Telling the Story: Qualitative Approaches to Measuring the Performance of Emerging Library Services." *Performance Measurement and Metrics* 9, no. 1: 7–17.

Bryant, Antony, and Kathy Charmaz, eds. 2010. *The SAGE Handbook of Grounded Theory.* Los Angeles: Sage.

Bryant, J. E. "An Ethnographic Study of User Behavior in Open3 at the Pilkington Library, Loughborough University." MSc dissertation, Loughborough University, Leicestershire, UK.

Bryant, Joanna. 2009. What Are Students Doing in Our Library? Ethnography as a Method of Exploring Library User Behaviour. *Library & Information Research* 33, no. 103: 3–9.

Burns, Vicki, and Kenn Harper. 2007. "Asking Students about Their Research." In *Studying Students: The Undergraduate Research Project at the University of Rochester,* ed. Nancy Fried Foster and Susan L. Gibbons. Chicago: Association of College and Research Libraries, 7–15.

Callinan, Joanne E. 2005. "Information-Seeking Behaviour of Undergraduate Biology Students: A Comparative Analysis of First Year and Final Year Students in University College Dublin." *Library Review* 54, no. 2: 86–99.

Campos, Cidhinnia M. Torres, Jean S. Phinney, Norma Perez-Brena, Chami Kim, Beatriz Ornelas, Liron Nemanim, Delia M. Padilla Kallemeyn, Anita Mihecoby, and Cinthya Ramirez. 2009. "A Mentor-Based Targeted Intervention for High-Risk Latino College Freshmen." *Journal of Hispanic Higher Education* 8, no. 2: 158–78.

Carey, Nancy, and Natalie M. Justh. 2004. National Center for Education Statistics, U.S. Department of Education. "Academic Libraries: 2000." NCES 2004-317.

Carlson, Scott. 2009. "Is It a Library? A Student Center? The Athenaeum Opens at Goucher College." *Chronicle of Higher Education* 56, no. 4: A16–17.

———. 2005. "The Library of the Future." *Chronicle of Higher Education* 52, no. 16: B23–.

CIBER (Centre for Information Behaviour and Evaluation of Research). 2008. *Information Behaviour of the Researcher of the Future: A CIBER Briefing Paper.* London: CIBER.

Connaway, Lynn Silipigni, and Thomas Dickey. 2010. "The Digital Information Seeker: Report on Findings from Selected OCLC, RIN and JISC User Behaviour Projects." OCLC Research.

Conway, Jan, Tania Olsson, and Nick Veale. 2009. "Make the Numbers Count: Improving Students' Learning Experiences." *SCONUL Focus* 45: 90–93.

Crabtree, A., D. M. Nichols, O. B. Jon, M. Rouncefield, and M. B. Twidale. 1998. "The Contribution of Ethnomethodologically-Informed Ethnography to the Process of Designing Digital Libraries." Lancaster: University of Lancaster Technical Report CSEG/5/98: 28.

Crabtree, A., D. M. Nichols, J. O'Brien, M. Rouncefield, and M. B. Twidale. 2000. "Ethnomethodologically Informed Ethnography and Information System Design." *Journal of the American Society for Information Science* 51, no. 7: 666–82.

Crabtree, A., M. B. Twidale, J. O'Brien, and D. M. Nichols. 1997. "Talking in the Library: Implications for the Design of Digital Libraries." In *Proceedings of the Second ACM International Conference on Digital Libraries*, 221–28.

DaCosta, Jacqui Weetman. 2010. "Is There an Information Literacy Skills Gap to Be Bridged? An Examination of Faculty Perceptions and Activities Relating to Information Literacy in the United States and England." *College & Research Libraries* 71, no. 3: 203–22.

Dayton, Boualoy, Nancy Gonzalez-Vasquez, Carla R. Martinez, and Caryn Plum. 2004. "Hispanic-Serving Institutions through the Eyes of Students and Administrators." *New Directions for Student Services* 105: 29–40.

De Rosa, C., J. Cantrell, D. Cellentani, J. Hawk, L. Jenkins, and A. Wilson. 2005. "College Students' Perceptions of Libraries and Information Resources: A Report to the OCLC Membership." Dublin, OH: OCLC Online Computer Library Center. http://www.oclc.org/us/en/reports/perceptionscollege.htm.

Delcore, H., J. Mullooly, J. Scroggins, and M. Scroggins. 2009. *The Library Study at Fresno State.* Fresno, CA: Institute of Public Anthropology, California State University, Fresno. http://www.csufresno.edu/anthropology/ipa/TheLibraryStudy(DelcoreMulloolyScroggins).pdf.

DePaul University, Office of Institutional Planning and Research. 2009. "Common Data Set." Chicago. http://oipr.depaul.edu/CDs/CDS.asp.

Dervin, B., L. S. Connaway, and C. Prabha. 2006. "Sense-Making the Information Confluence: The Whys and Hows of College and University User Satisfying of Information Needs." *Final Project Performance Report.* IMLS AWARD #LG-02-03-0062-03.

Dewey, Barbara I. 2008. "Social, Intellectual, and Cultural Spaces: Creating Compelling Library Environments for the Digital Age." *Journal of Library Administration* 48, no. 1 (2008): 85–94.

Dole, Wanda V., and Jitka M. Hurych. 2001. "Values for Librarians in the Information Age." *Journal of Information Ethics* 10, no. 2: 38–50.

Edgar, William B. 2007. "Toward a Theory of University Library Group Work: An Approach for Development." *Journal of Academic Librarianship* 33, no. 2: 268–75.

Elteto, Sharon, Rose M. Jackson, and Adriene Lim. 2008. "Is the Library a 'Welcoming Space'? An Urban Academic Library and Diverse Student Experiences." *Portal: Libraries and the Academy* 8, no. 3: 325–37.

Emerson, Robert M., Rachel I. Fretz, and Linda L. Shaw. 1995. *Writing Ethnographic Field Notes.* Chicago: University of Chicago Press.

Epperson, T. W. 2006. "Toward a Critical Ethnography of Librarian-Supported Collaborative Learning." *Library Philosophy and Practice* 9, no. 1: 1–14.

Faculty Senate of the University of Illinois at Chicago. n.d. "UIC Scope and Mission Statement." _UIC. http://www.uic.edu/index.html/admin_scope .shtml.

Fister, Barbara. 1992. "The Research Processes of Undergraduate Students." *Journal of Academic Librarianship* 18, no. 3: 163–69.

Flores, Javier. 2009. *Demographic Characteristics of Online Learners Enrolled at Community Colleges Designated Hispanic Serving Institutions.* http://dspace

.lib.ttu.edu/etd/bitstream/handle/2346/ETD-TTU-2009-12-236/FLORES
-DISSERTATION.pdf?sequence = 4.

Forrest, Charles, and Martin Halbert, eds. 2009. *A Field Guide to the Information Commons*. Lanham, MD: Scarecrow.

Forrest, Charles, et al. 2005. "Beyond Classroom Construction and Design." *Reference & User Services Quarterly* 44, no. 4: 296–300.

Forsythe, D. E. 1998. "Using Ethnography to Investigate Life Scientists' Information Needs." *Bulletin of the Medical Library Association* 86, no. 3: 402.

Foster, Nancy Fried, and Susan L. Gibbons. 2007. *Studying Students: The Undergraduate Research Project at the University of Rochester*. Chicago: Association of College and Research Libraries.

———. 2005. "Understanding Faculty to Improve Content Recruitment for Institutional Repositories." *D-Lib Magazine* 11, no. 1. http://www.dlib.org/dlib/january05/foster/01foster.html.

Freeman, Geoffrey T. 2005. *The Library as Place: Changes in Learning Patterns, Collections, Technology, and Use*. Washington, DC: Council on Library and Information Resources.

Freiburger, Gary. 2010. "Introduction: Be Prepared." *Journal of the Medical Library Association* 98, no. 1: 24–.

Gabridge, T., M. Gaskell, and A. Stout. 2008. "Information Seeking through Students' Eyes: The MIT Photo Diary Study." *College & Research Libraries* 69, no. 6: 510.

Gamerman, Ellen, et al. 2007. "High Schools: How the Schools Stack Up." *Wall Street Journal.* http://online.wsj.com/public/resources/documents/info-COLLEGE0711-sort.html.

Gandara, Patricia, and Frances Contreras. 2009. *The Latino Education Crisis*. Cambridge, MA: Harvard University Press.

Garcia, Maricela, Beatrice Ponce De Leon, Benjamin Osborne, and Adriana Moreno Nevdiez. 2008. "An American Agenda from a Latino Perspective." Latino Policy Forum. http://www.latinopolicyforum.org/assets/C0589015_LatinosUnited_v3_FINAL_VERSION.pdf.

Garrod, Andrew, Robert Kilkenny, and Christina Gomez. 2007. *Mi Voz, Mi Vida*. Ithaca, NY: Cornell University Press.

Gayton, Jeffrey T. 2008. "Academic Libraries: 'Social' or 'Communal'? The Nature and Future of Academic Libraries." *Journal of Academic Librarianship* 34, no. 1: 60–66.

Geertz, Clifford. 1988. *Works and Lives: The Anthropologist as Author*. Stanford, CA: Stanford University Press.

———. 1983. *Local Knowledge: Further Essays in Interpretive Anthropology*. New York: Basic Books.

Glaser, Barney, and Anselm Strauss. 1967. *The Discovery of Grounded Theory: Strategies for Qualitative Research*. Chicago: Aldine.

Gonzalez, Kenneth P., Jennifer E. Jovel, and Carla Stoner. 2004. "Latinas: The New Latino Majority in College." *New Directions for Student Services* 105: 17–27.

Grassian, Esther S., and Joan R. Kaplowitz. 2009. *Information Literacy Instruction: Theory and Practice*. 2nd ed. New York: Neal-Schuman.

Griffiths, J. R., and P. Brophy. 2005. "Student Searching Behavior and the Web: Use of Academic Resources and Google." *Trends* 53, no. 4: 539.

Gross, Linda S. 2004. "Creating Meaning from Intersections of Career and Cultural Identity." *New Directions for Student Services* 105: 63–77.

Hampton-Reeves, S., C. Mashiter, J. Westaway, P. Lumsden, H. Day, and H. Hewertson. 2009. *Students' Use of Research Content in Teaching and Learning*. A report for the Joint Information Systems Council (JISC). Centre for Research-Informed Teaching, University of Central Lancashire.

Haras, C., E. A. Lopez, and K. Ferry. 2008. "(Generation 1.5) Latino Students and the Library: A Case Study." *Journal of Academic Librarianship* 34, no. 5: 425–33.

Harloe, Bart, and Helene Williams. 2009. "The College Library in the 21st Century." *College and Research Libraries News* 70, no. 9: 514–35.

Head, Alison J., and Michael Eisenberg. 2009. *How College Students Seek Information in the Digital Age*. Project Information Literacy Progress Report. University of Washington.

Hinchliffe, L. J., and M. Oakleaf. 2010. "Sustainable Progress through Impact: The Value of Academic Libraries Project." In *Proceedings of the World Library and Information Congress: 76th IFLA General Conference and Assembly*, 1–7. http://www.ifla.org/files/hq/papers/ifla76/72-hinchliffe -en.pdf.

Hobbs, K., and D. Klare. 2010. "User Driven Design: Using Ethnographic Techniques to Plan Student Study Space." *Technical Services Quarterly* 27, no. 4: 347–63.

Holland, D. C., and M. A. Eisenhart. 1990. *Educated in Romance: Women, Achievement, and College Culture*. Chicago: University of Chicago Press.

Institute for Latino Studies, University of Notre Dame. 2008. "Latino Educational Equity: A Web-Based Index and Compendium of Best Practices in Latino Education in the United States." http://latinostudies.nd.edu/pubs/pubs/ LatinoEdEquityIndexWeb.pdf.

Jahn, N. 2008. "Anthropologically Motivated Usability Evaluation: An Exploration of IREON–International Relations and Area Studies Gateway." *Library Hi Tech* 26, no. 4: 606–21.

Jankowska, Maria Anna, and James W. Marcum. 2010. "Sustainability Challenge for Academic Libraries: Planning for the Future." *College & Research Libraries* 71, no. 2: 160–70.

Koehler, Wallace C., Jitka M. Hurych, Wanda V. Dole, and Joanna Wall. 2000. "Ethical Values of Information and Library Professionals: An Expanded Analysis." *International Information and Library Review* 32, no. 3/4: 485–507.

Kuh, George D., and Robert M. Gonyea. 2003. "The Role of the Academic Library in Promoting Student Engagement in Learning." *College & Research Libraries* 64, no. 4: 256–63.

Kyrillidou, Martha, and Les Bland. 2009. *Association of Research Libraries Statistics 2007–2008.* Washington, DC: Association of Research Libraries.

Lee, H. L. 2008. "Information Structures and Undergraduate Students." *Journal of Academic Librarianship* 34, no. 3: 211–19.

Lewis, David W. 2007. "A Strategy for Academic Libraries in the First Quarter of the 21st Century." *College & Research Libraries* 68, no. 5: 418–34.

Lopez, Mark Hugo. 2009. "Latinos and Education: Explaining the Attainment Gap." Pew Hispanic Center. http://pewhispanic.org/files/reports/115.pdf.

Maestas, Ricardo, Gloria S. Vaquera, and Linda Munoz Zehr. 2007. "Factors Impacting Sense of Belonging at a Hispanic-Serving Institution." *Journal of Hispanic Higher Education* 6, no. 3: 237–56.

Martell, Charles. 2008. "The Absent User: Physical Use of Academic Library Collections and Services Continues to Decline 1995–2006." *Journal of Academic Librarianship* 34, no. 5: 400–407.

Martinez, Magadelena, and Edith Fernandez. 2004. "Latinos at Community Colleges." *New Directions for Student Services* 105: 51–62.

McClanahan, Kitty, Lei Wu, Carol Tenopir, and Donald W. King. 2010. "Embracing Change: Perceptions of E-Journals by Faculty Members." *Learned Publishing* 23, no. 3: 209–23.

McKnight, Michelynn. 2001. "Beyond Surveys: Methods for Finding Out 'Why?'" *Journal of Hospital Librarianship* 1, no. 2: 31–39.

Mellon, Constance A. 1986. "Library Anxiety: A Grounded Theory and Its Development." *College & Research Libraries* 47, no. 2: 160–65.

Millet, Michelle S., and Clint Chamberlain. 2007. "Word-of-Mouth Marketing Using Peer Tutors." *Serials Librarian* 53, no. 3: 95.

Mina, Liliana, Jose A. Cabrales, Cynthia M. Juarez, and Fernando Rodriguez-Vasquez. 2004. "Support Programs That Work." *New Directions for Student Services* 105: 79–88.

Moffatt, M. 1989. *Coming of Age in New Jersey: College and American Culture.* New Brunswick, NJ: Rutgers University Press.

Mooney, Margarita, and Deborah Rivas-Drake. 2008. "Colleges Need to Recognize, and Serve, the 3 Kinds of Latino Students." *Chronicle of Higher Education* 54, no. 29: A37–A39.

Moore, Anne C., and Gary Ivory. 2003. "Do Hispanic-Serving Institutions Have What It Takes to Foster Information Literacy? One Case." *Journal of Latinos and Education* 2, no. 4: 217–27.

Nahl, D. 1998. "Ethnography of Novices' First Use of Web Search Engines." *Internet Reference Services Quarterly* 3, no. 2: 51–72.

NASPA Foundation. 2008. "Profile of Today's College Student." http://www.naspa.org/divctr/research/profile/results.cfm.

Nathan, R. 2005. *My Freshman Year: What a Professor Learned by Becoming a Student.* Ithaca, NY: Cornell University Press.

Neal, James G. 2009. "What Do Users Want? What Do Users Need? W(h)ither the Academic Research Library?" *Journal of Library Administration* 49, no. 5: 463–68.

Newman, John Henry. 2007. "The Idea of a University." http://www.newman reader.org.

Northeastern Illinois University, Office of Institutional Research. 2009. "Common Data Set." Chicago. http://www.neiu.edu/~isp/Common%20 Data%20Set.html.

Novotny, Eric. 2002. *Reference Service Statistics and Assessment: A SPEC Kit,* ed. Lee Ann George. Washington, DC: Association of Research Libraries.

Nyce, J. M., and N. P. Thomas. 1999. "Can a 'Hard' Science Answer 'Hard' Questions? A Response to Sandstrom and Sandstrom." *Library Quarterly* 69, no. 2: 295–98.

Ortiz, Anna M. 2004. "Promoting the Success of Latino Students: A Call to Action." *New Directions for Student Services* 105: 89–97.

Oseguera, Leticia, Angela M. Locks, and Irene I. Vega. 2009. "Increasing Latina/o Students' Baccalaureate Attainment: A Focus on Retention." *Journal of Hispanic Higher Education* 8, no. 1: 23–53.

Ostrander, Margaret. 2008. "Talking, Looking, Flying, Searching: Information Seeking Behaviour in Second Life." *Library Hi Tech* 26, no. 4: 512–24.

Othman, R. 2004. "An Applied Ethnographic Method for Evaluating Retrieval Features." *Electronic Library* 22, no. 5: 425–32.

Passel, Jeffrey, and Paul Taylor. 2009. "Who's Hispanic?" http://pewhispanic
.org/files/reports/111.pdf.

Persily, Gail L., and Karen A. Butter. 2010. *Reinvisioning and Redesigning "a
Library for the Fifteenth through Twenty-First Centuries": A Case Study on Loss
of Space from the Library and Center for Knowledge Management, University of
California, San Francisco.* Vol. 98. Medical Library Association.

Phan, T., L. Hardesty, C. Sheckells, and D. Davis. 2009. National Center for
Education Statistics, Institute of Education Sciences, U.S. Department of
Education. "Academic Libraries: 2008." NCES 2010–348.

Prabha, C., L. S. Connaway, and T. J. Dickey. 2006. *The Whys and Hows of
College and University User Satisficing of Information Needs: Phase IV Report:
Semi-Structured Interview Study.* Report on National Leadership Grant LG-02-
03-0062-03, to Institute of Museum and Library Services, Washington, DC.
Columbus, Ohio: School of Communication, Ohio State University. http://
imlsproject.comm.ohio-state.edu/imls_reports/imls_PH_IV_report_list.html.

Pritchard, Sarah M. 2008. "Deconstructing the Library: Reconceptualizing
Collections, Spaces and Services." *Journal of Library Administration* 48, no. 2:
219–33.

Project Information Literacy: A Large-Scale Study about Early Adults and Their
Research Habits. http://projectinfolit.org.

Ranganathan, S. R. 1963. *The Five Laws of Library Science.* New York: Asia.

Roberts, Susan, and Margaret Weaver. 2006. "Spaces for Learners and Learning:
Evaluating the Impact of Technology-Rich Learning Spaces." *New Review of
Academic Librarianship* 12, no. 2: 95–107.

Robinson, Catherine M., and Peter Reid. 2007. "Do Academic Enquiry Services
Scare Students?" *Reference Services Review* 35, no. 3: 405–24.

Ruppel, Margie, and Jody Condit Fagan. 2002. "Instant Messaging Reference:
Users' Evaluation of Library Chat." *Reference Services Review* 30, no. 3:
183–97.

Sanchez, Bernadette. 2006. "Making It in College: The Value of Significant
Individuals in the Lives of Mexican American Adolescents." *Journal of
Hispanic Higher Education* 5, no. 1: 48–67.

Sandstrom, Alan R., and Pamela Effrein Sandstrom. 1999. "Antiscientific
Approaches to the Study of Social Life: A Response to Thomas and Nyce."
Library Quarterly 69, no. 2: 299.

———. 1998. "Science and Nonscience in Qualitative Research: A Response to
Thomas and Nyce." *Library Quarterly* 68, no. 2: 249–54.

———. 1995. "The Use and Misuse of Anthropological Methods in Library and
Information Science Research." *Library Quarterly* 65, no. 2: 161–99.

Santiago, Deborah. 2009. "Enrolling vs. Serving Latino Students." *Diverse: Issues in Higher Education* 26, no. 16: 20.

Santiago, Deborah A., and Sally J. Andrade. 2010. "Emerging Hispanic-Serving Institutions(HSIs): Serving Latino Students." Excelencia in Education. http://www.edexcelencia.org/system/files/Emerging_HSI.pdf.

Santiago, Deborah A., and Travis Reindl. 2009. "Taking Stock: Higher Education and Latinos." Excelencia in Education. http://www.edexcelencia.org/system/files/ExcelenciaTakingStock.pdf.

Seadle, Michael. 2007. "Anthropologists in the Library: A Review of Studying Students." *Library Hi Tech* 25, no. 4: 612–19.

———. 2000. "Project Ethnography: An Anthropological Approach to Assessing Digital Library Services." *Library Trends* 49, no. 2: 370–85.

Sens, Thomas. 2009. "Twelve Keys to Library Design." *Library Journal* 9 (May 15): 34–.

Shapiro, Harold T. 2005. *A Larger Sense of Purpose: Higher Education and Society.* Princeton, NJ: Princeton University Press.

Shear, Michael. 2010. "Obama Speech Ties U.S. Need for More College Graduates to the Economic Recovery." *Washington Post*, August 9, 2010. http://www.washingtonpost.com/wp-dyn/content/article/2010/08/09/AR2010080904278.html.

Shill, Harold B., and Shawn Tonner. 2004. "Does the Building Still Matter? Usage Patterns in New, Expanded, and Renovated Libraries, 1995–2002." *College & Research Libraries* 65, no. 2: 123–50.

———. 2003. "Creating a Better Place: Physical Improvements in Academic Libraries, 1995–2002." *College & Research Libraries* 64, no. 6: 431–66.

Shumar, Wesley. 2004. "Making Strangers at Home: Anthropologists Studying Higher Education." *Journal of Higher Education* 75, no. 1: 23–41.

Slouka, Mark. 2009. "Dehumanized: When Math and Science Rule the School." *Harper's Magazine,* September, 32–40.

Sobel, Karen. 2009. "Promoting Library Reference Services to First-Year Undergraduate Students: What Works?" *Reference & User Services Quarterly* 48, no. 4: 362–71.

Stearns, Christina, Satoshi Watanabe, National Center for Education Statistics. 2002. *Hispanic Serving Institutions: Statistical Trends from 1990 to 1999.*

Stern, Gary M. 2009. "Why Latino Students Are Failing to Attend College." *Education Digest* 75, no. 1: 46–49.

Stoffle, Carla J., and Cheryl Cuillier. "Student-Centered Service and Support: A Case Study of the University of Arizona Libraries' Information Commons. *Journal of Library Administration* 50, no. 2: 117–34.

Suarez, D. 2007. "What Students Do When They Study in the Library: Using Ethnographic Methods to Observe Student Behavior." *Electronic Journal of Academic and Special Librarianship* 8, no. 3.

Swope, Mary J., and Jeffrey Katzer. 1972. "Why Don't They Ask Questions? The Silent Majority." *RQ* 12, no. 2: 161–66.

Thomas, N. P., and J. M. Nyce. 1998. "Qualitative Research in LIS: Redux: A Response to a [Re] Turn to Positivistic Ethnography." *Library Quarterly* 68, no. 1: 108–13.

Torres, Vasti. 2004. "The Diversity among Us: Puerto Ricans, Cuban Americans, Caribbean Americans, and Central and South Americans." *New Directions for Student Services* 105: 5–16.

Tyckoson, David A. 2000. "Library Service for the First-Generation College Student." In *Teaching the New Library to Today's Users,* ed. Trudi E. Jacobson and Helen C. Williams. New York: Neal-Schuman, 89–105.

UIC Office of Institutional Research. 2009. "Common Data Set." Chicago. http://www.oir.uic.edu/commondataset/index.asp.

———. 2010. "Racial/Ethnic Distribution: Undergraduates." http://www.dria.uic.edu/quickfacts/default.asp?rpttopic=distribution.

UIC Office of the Vice Chancellor for Student Affairs. 2002. "Who Are the First-Generation Students at UIC? An Examination of the Fall 2002 Beginning Freshman Class." http://tigger.uic.edu/~ardinger/assessment/parent-ed.html.

UIC Office of the Vice Provost for Academic and Enrollment Services and Office of the Vice Chancellor for Student Affairs. 2009. "Special Comparison Report from the 2009 Administration of the UIC Entering Student Survey—Students from Chicago Public Schools." http://www.vcsa.uic.edu/MainSite/departments/SA+Research+and+Assessment/events/.

U.S. Department of Education. 2010. *Developing Hispanic-Serving Institutions Program—Title V: Definition of Hispanic-Serving Institutions.*

———. National Center for Education Statistics website. http://nces.ed.gov/fastfacts/display.asp?id=37.

U.S. Department of Labor. Bureau of Labor Statistics website. http://www.bls.gov/bls/inflation.htm.

Villalpando, Octavio. 2004. "Practical Considerations of Critical Race Theory and Latino Critical Theory for Latino College Students." *New Directions for Student Services* 105: 41–50.

Vondracek, Ruth. 2007. "Comfort and Convenience? Why Students Choose Alternatives to the Library." *Portal: Libraries and the Academy* 7 , no. 3: 277–93.

Wallace, Amy. 2007. "Lifelong Information Literacy in Southern California." *Educator's Spotlight Digest* 2, no. 3: 16–20.

Weaver, Joyce. 1999. "Point. Click. Matriculate: Corporate Influence in the University and the Academic Library." *Libri* 49, no. 3: 142–49.

Webb, Kathleen M., Molly A. Schaller, and Sawyer A. Hunley. "Measuring Library Space Use and Preferences: Charting a Path toward Increased Engagement." *Portal: Libraries and the Academy* 8, no. 4: 407–22.

"What's a College for?" 1932. *Saturday Evening Post,* January 30, p. 20.

Whitlatch, Jo Bell. 2001. "Evaluating Reference Services: A Practical Guide." *Library Mosaics* 12, no. 6: 21.

Whitmire, Ethelene. 2003. "Cultural Diversity and Undergraduates' Academic Library Use." *Journal of Academic Librarianship* 29, no. 3: 148–53.

Wong, William, Hanna Stelmaszewska, Nazlin Bhimani, Sukhbinder Barn, and Balbir Barn. 2009. "User Behaviour in Resource Discovery: Final Report." JISC.

Zalaquett, Carlos P. 2006. "Study of Successful Latina/o Students." *Journal of Hispanic Higher Education* 5, no. 1: 35–47.

CONTRIBUTORS

ANDREW D. ASHER was the lead research anthropologist for the ERIAL Project. He holds a PhD in sociocultural anthropology from the University of Illinois at Urbana-Champaign and is currently a Council on Library and Information Resources fellow for scholarly communications at Bucknell University, where he is conducting research on faculty publications practices and continuing his inquiries into scholarly search processes.

LYNDA M. DUKE is associate professor, academic outreach librarian at Illinois Wesleyan University. Her responsibilities include coordinating assessment and marketing activities for the library, as well as collection development and library instruction for the departments of Hispanic studies, economics, and business administration. She served as principal investigator for the IWU research team of the ERIAL Project. She earned her master's degree in library and information science from the University of Illinois at Urbana-Champaign and her master's of urban planning from the University of Michigan.

ANNIE ARMSTRONG is an assistant librarian and assistant professor and coordinator of library instruction at the Richard J. Daley Library at the University of Illinois at Chicago. Her research interests include instructional methods for undergraduate researchers and interactive online learning.

AMANDA BINDER is a visiting instructional services librarian at the University of Illinois at Springfield. She received her BA in sociology from Bard College and her MS in library and information science from the University of Illinois Urbana-Champaign. Previously she worked as a graduate assistant at the undergraduate library at the University of Illinois Urbana-Champaign.

DAVID GREEN is the associate university librarian for collections and information services at Northeastern Illinois University. He holds a master's of science degree in information systems from DePaul University in Chicago and a master's in library science from Indiana University, Bloomington. He has previously held positions at Loyola University in Chicago, Roosevelt University, and Temple University in Japan. Over the years, Green has written and been awarded several grants. Most recently, he was the grant coordinator and project manager for the ERIAL Project.

FIROUZEH LOGAN is a reference librarian at the University of Illinois at Chicago. Her research interests include the history and practice of public services in libraries, specifically reference and instruction in academia.

SUSAN MILLER is the resident anthropologist for the Chicago libraries of the ERIAL Project. She has an MA in the social sciences from the University of Chicago. Her previous work has been in evaluation of mental health and substance abuse treatment programs for homeless women.

NANCY SARAH MURILLO is the library instruction coordinator at Northeastern Illinois University. She holds a master's degree in information and library science from Dominican University, and a master's in Latin American literatures and cultures from Northeastern Illinois University. Murillo's professional interests include Latin American literatures, Latino culture, and information literacy.

ELIZABETH PICKARD is a reference librarian at the University of Illinois at Chicago.

NATALIE TAGGE is visiting instructional services librarian at the University of Illinois at Springfield. She received her BA in anthropology from Occidental College and her MS in library and information science from the University of Illinois at Urbana-Champaign. She previously worked as state virtual reference coordinator at the Illinois State Library, as a graduate assistant at the University of Illinois Urbana-Champaign's Chemistry Library, and taught high school students as an Americorps volunteer.

MARY THILL is humanities librarian at Northeastern Illinois University. She holds an MLIS from Dominican University and an MA from the University of Illinois at Chicago.

JANE B. TREADWELL is university librarian and dean of library instructional services at the University of Illinois at Springfield. A past president of the Illinois Association of College and Research Libraries, she has also served in leadership positions in the Association for Library Collections and Technical Services. Her past publications and presentations have focused on the subjects of collection development and acquisitions, organizational change in libraries, and library marketing.

INDEX

A

Academic Search Premier (database), 74
analysis strategies, ERIAL project, 12–13
applied anthropology, 5
Armstrong, Annie, 13, 31–48
Asher, Andrew D.
    conclusions and future research, 161–167, 164
    ERIAL project, 1–14
    student research behavior, 71–85
AskAmes, 146
assessment and marketing changes, 155–156
assistants, student, 158–159
Association of College and Research Libraries (ACRL), 19, 33

B

Beaver, William, 18
behaviors
    help-seeking, 49–70
    student research, 71–85
Bennett, Scott, 128
Binder, Amanda, 14, 127–142, 164
Blum, Susan, 5
Bok, Derek, 17–18

C

changes, assessment and marketing, 155–156
CINAHL (database), 77
co-viewing process, analysis strategy, 12
cognitive maps, 11
"College and the Well-Lived Life" (Bok), 17
Comfort, William Wistar, 22–23
Coming of Age in New Jersey (Moffatt study), 5
communication methods, 43
"Creating a Better Place" (Shill and Tonner), 128

D

databases
    choosing, 74–76
    CINAHL, 77
    JSTOR, 64, 74–76, 115
    PsycINFO, 37, 74
    search construction, 76–80
DePaul University, 2, 52
Developing Academic Leadership through Engagement (DALE), 101
diaries, mapping, 10

"Do We Need More College
Graduates?"(Beaver), 18
"Does the Building Still Matter?"
(Shill and Tonner), 128
Duke, Lynda
conclusions and future research,
161–167
student information searching,
13–14
student research behavior, 71–85
transformative changes, 143–160

E
EBSCO Discovery Service, 154–155
Educated in Romance (Holland and
Eisenhart study), 5
Eisenhart, Margaret, 5
ERIAL project
analysis strategies, 12–13
background, 5–8
ethnographic approach, 3–5
methodology, 8–12
study introduction, 1–5
study organization, 13–14
transformative changes and,
144–148
ethnographic interviews, 8, 10–11, 73
Ethnographic Research in Illinois
Academic Libraries (ERIAL),
1–14, 144–148
ethnographic study of libraries, 5
ethnography, defined, 3

F
faculty and librarian relationships,
38–40
*A Field Guide to the Information
Commons* (Forrest and Halbert),
128
first-generation students. *See* students,
first-generation
First Year Experience (FYE) program,
67
Forrest, Charles, 128

Foster, Nancy Fried, 6
Freeman, Geoffrey T., 128
Fresno State University, 6

G
Gibbons, Susan, 6
Grassian, Esther, 32
Green, David, 1–14, 87–108, 163

H
Halbert, Martin, 128
Haverford College, 23
help-seeking behaviors
answers to, 66–69
behavior and relationships, 50–52
data and methods, 52
discussion, 65–66
knowing when to access help,
64–65
librarians, relationships with,
53–55
not seeking help, 62–63
peers and family, seeking help
from, 58–60
professors, seeking help from,
55–58
public libraries and, 62
relationships, lacking university
supports for, 60–62
results, 52–53
self-reliance and, 63–64
study conclusions, 69–70
study introduction, 49–50
Hispanic-Serving Institution, defined,
94–95
Hispanic students
defining, 88–89
family and geography, 97–98
general trends, 95
learning about, 90–92
librarian awareness, 103
librarians, connecting with,
104–107
library resource workshops, 98

Maria's story, 92–94
NEIU and Hispanic institutions, 94–95
peer support, 100–103
personal relationships, 95–97
retention of, 103–104
seeking help, 98–100
study conclusions, 107–108
study introduction, 87–88
Hispanic students, retention, 103–104
Holland, Dorothy, 5

I
The Idea of a University (Newman), 17
idealism, pragmatism and, 15–30
ILLiad (website), 74, 82, 154
Illinois Wesleyan University (IWU), 2
information commons, 127–128
Information Literacy: Theory and Practice (Grassian and Kaplowitz), 32
Information Literacy Competency Standards, 19
instructional services, marketing. See marketing instructional services
interviews, research process, 10–11, 73

J
journals, research, 10
JSTOR (database), 64, 74–76, 115

K
Kaplowitz, Joan, 32

L
Latino students. See Hispanic students
learning commons, 128
LibQual+ (survey), 131, 133
librarians
    faculty relationships with, 38–30
    help seeking behaviors and, 53–55
    Hispanic student relationships with, 104–107

instruction time for, 32–33
as liaisons, 44–47
marketing instructional services and, 36–38
understanding role, 49–54
library anxiety, 51
The Library as Place (Freeman), 128
library liaison model, 152–153
Library of Congress, 34, 72
"Library Service for the First-Generation College Student," 111
Library Services and Technology Act, 2, 109
library spaces
    background, 129–132
    cognitive mapping and, 134–135
    design workshops, 10, 136–137
    flip charts, 137–138
    interviews and photo diaries, 138–140
    student preferences in, 133–134
    study conclusions, 140–142
    study introduction, 127–129
Lindahl, Dave, 6
Logan, Firouzeh, 13, 109–125, 163

M
"Make the Numbers Count" (study), 110
mapping diaries, 10
marketing and assessment changes. See transformative changes
marketing instructional services
    barriers to, 40–42
    enhancing library instruction, 38–40
    faculty impressions, 35–36
    liaison relationships and, 44–47
    librarian assistance and, 36–38
    library instruction, importance of, 32–33
    outreach and communication, 42–44

marketing instructional services (cont.)
    scope and methodology, 33
    student perceptions, 34–35
    study conclusion, 47–48
    study introduction, 31–32
Massachusetts Institute of
    Technology, 6
McKnight, Michelynn, 110
Mellon, Constance, 51
mentors, peer, 67–69, 101
methodology, ERIAL project, 8–12
Miller, Susan, 1–14, 49–70, 164
Moffatt, Michael, 5
Murillo, Nancy, 13, 49–70
My Freshman Year (Nathan study), 5
My Word! (Blum study), 5

N
Nathan, Rebekah, 5
Newman, John Henry (Cardinal), 17
Northeastern Illinois University
    (NEIU), 2, 52
Northern Arizona University, 5

O
Objectives for Information Literacy
    Instruction, 34
OCLC summary of user behavior, 72
Office of Institutional Research (OIR),
    90–92

P
peer mentors, 67–69, 101
photo journals, 9
Pickard, Elizabeth, 13, 109–125, 163
"Point. Click. Matriculate" (Weaver),
    17
pragmatism and idealism
    background, 17–19
    discussion, 21–27
    methods of, 19–20
    study conclusions, 27–30
    study introduction, 15–16
Princeton University, 17

Profile of Today's College Student
    (survey), 16
programs, changes in. See
    transformative changes
Project Information Literacy, 33, 83
PsycINFO (database), 37, 74

R
reference versus research assistant,
    145
research, future and conclusions
    conducting studies, 164–165
    future in, 165–166
    study introduction, 161–164
    summary, 167
research behavior
    database, choosing, 74–76
    search construction, 76–80
    seeking help, 83
    source evaluation, 80–82
    study conclusions, 84–85
    study introduction, 71–74
    technical problems, 82–83
research tools, using, 34
retrospective interviews, 11
Ronald Williams Library (Illinois), 6
Rutgers University (New Jersey), 5

S
Seadle, Michael, 110
services, changes in. See
    transformative changes
services, marketing of. See marketing
    instructional services
Shapiro, Harold, 17
Shill, Harold B., 128
Small, Cathy, 5
space design workshops, 10, 136–137
student assistants, training, 158–159
students, first-generation
    background, 110–112
    communication and, 123
    methodology, 112–113
    number, source selection, 116–118

obstacles in, 120
obtaining help, 120–123
pre-college, 113
searching, 114–116
study conclusions, 123–125
study introduction, 109–110
type, source selection, 118–120
*Studying Students: The Undergraduate
     Research Project,* 110

T
Tagge, Natalie, 14, 127–142, 164
Thill, Mary, 13, 15–30
Tonner, Shawn, 128
training student assistants, 158–159
transformative changes
     5 areas of change, 151
     ERIAL project and, 144–148
     identifying and selecting, 148–151
     information literacy, 156–158
     marketing and assessment,
          155–156
     relationship strengthening,
          151–153
     student training, 158–159
     study conclusions, 159–160
     study introduction, 143–144
     web pages and websites, 153–155

Treadwell, Jane, 13–14, 127–142,
     164
Trinity University (Texas), 67

U
University of Illinois at Chicago
     (UIC), 2, 52
University of Illinois at Springfield
     (UIS), 2
University of Rochester (New York), 6

V
"The Value of Academic Libraries
     Project," 33

W
Weaver, Joyce, 17
web design workshops, 10
web pages, changes to. *See*
     transformative changes
Wesleyan University, 6
Whitlatch, Jo Bell, 123
"Who Are the First-Generation
     Students at UIC" (study), 111
workshops
     library resource, 98
     library space design, 136–137
     web and space design, 10

You may also be interested in

REFLECTIVE TEACHING, EFFECTIVE LEARNING
Instructional Literacy for Library Educators
Char Booth

Laying the foundation for effective teaching, Booth outlines a four-part framework of Instructional Literacy, which includes Reflective Practice, Educational Theory, Teaching Technologies, and Instructional Design.

PRINT ISBN: 978-0-8389-1052-8
EBOOK: 7400-0528
PRINT/EBOOK BUNDLE: 7700-0528
208 PAGES / 8.5" X 11"

TEACHING INFORMATION LITERACY
JOANNA M. BURKHARDT AND MARY C. MACDONALD WITH ANDRÉE J. RATHEMACHER
ISBN: 978-0-8389-1053-5

THE FACULTY COMMONS
D. RUSSELL BAILEY, PHD
ISBN: 978-0-8389-1115-0

OPEN ACCESS
WALT CRAWFORD
ISBN: 978-0-8389-1106-8

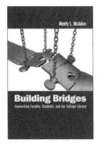

BUILDING BRIDGES
MONTY L. MCADOO
ISBN: 978-0-8389-1019-1

INTERLIBRARY LOAN PRACTICES HANDBOOK, 3E
EDITED BY CHERIÉ L. WEIBLE & KAREN L. JANKE
ISBN: 978-0-8389-1081-8

WEB-BASED INSTRUCTION, 3E
SUSAN SHARPLESS SMITH
ISBN: 978-0-8389-1056-6

CPSIA information can be obtained at www.ICGtesting.com
Printed in the USA
LVOW010554211212

312701LV00004B/11/P

9 780838 911167